HANBALI ACTS OF WORSHIP

HANBALI ACTS OF WORSHIP

From Ibn Balbān's
The Supreme Synopsis

Akhṣar al-Mukhtaṣarāt

MUSA FURBER

Updated June 5, 2020

ISBN 978-1-944904-03-6 (paper)

Published by:
Islamosaic
islamosaic.com
publications@islamosaic.com

بسم الله الرحمن الرحيم

All praise is to Allah alone, the Lord of the Worlds
And may He send His benedictions upon
our master Muhammad, his Kin
and his Companions
and grant them
peace

TRANSLITERATION KEY

ء	ʾ (1)	ر	r(6)	ف	f
ا	ā, a	ز	z	ق	q(13)
ب	b	س	s	ك	k
ت	t	ش	sh	ل	l
ث	th(2)	ص	ṣ(7)	م	m
ج	j	ض	ḍ(8)	ن	n
ح	ḥ(3)	ط	ṭ(9)	ه	h(14)
خ	kh(4)	ظ	ẓ(10)	و	ū, u, w
د	d	ع	ʿ (11)	ي	ī, i, y
ذ	dh(5)	غ	gh(12)		

1. A distinctive glottal stop made at the bottom of the throat.
2. Pronounced like the *th* in *think*.
3. Hard *h* sound made at the Adam's apple in the middle of the throat.
4. Pronounced like *ch* in Scottish *loch*.
5. Pronounced like *th* in *this*.
6. A slightly trilled *r* made behind the upper front teeth.
7. An emphatic *s* pronounced behind the upper front teeth.
8. An emphatic *d*-like sound made by pressing the entire tongue against the upper palate.
9. An emphatic *t* sound produced behind the front teeth.
10. An emphatic *th* sound, like the *th* in *this*, made behind the front teeth.
11. A distinctive Semitic sound made in the middle of the throat and sounding to a Western ear more like a vowel than a consonant.
12. A guttural sound made at the top of the throat resembling the untrilled German and French *r*.
13. A hard *k* sound produced at the back of the palate.
14. This sound is like the English *h* but has more body. It is made at the very bottom of the throat and pronounced at the beginning, middle, and ends of words.

CONTENTS

المُحْتَوَيَاتُ

TRANSLITERATION KEY VI
CONVENTIONS VIII
PREFACE IX
INTRODUCTION 1
1 Purification 3
2 Prayer 23
3 Funerals 62
4 Zakat 72
5 Fasting 81
6 Pilgrimage 88
7 Jihad 109
BIBLIOGRAPHY 115
DETAILED TABLE OF CONTENTS 116

CONVENTIONS

الْمُصْطَلَحَاتُ

Readers should be familiar with the following terms:

- *Wājib* – something one is censured for omitting, categorically. Throughout this translation, it is usually rendered as "obligatory."
- *Farḍ* – something established via incontrovertible evidence. It has been rendered as "prescribed."
- *Ḥarām* – something one is legally censured for, including utterances and acts of the heart. It has been rendered as "unlawful."
- *Mandūb, mustaḥabb, sunnah* – something one is rewarded for performing, yet one is not punished for neglecting it, categorically. It includes utterances and actions of the heart, and has been rendered as "recommended."
- *Makrūh* – is that which someone is praised for avoiding yet is not censured for performing. It has been rendered as "disliked."
- *Mubāḥ, ḥalāl* – something that in and of itself is free of praise and censure. It has been rendered as "permissible."

PREFACE

الْمُقَدِّمَة

While studying in Damascus, I was blessed with the opportunity to study Hanbali fiqh for three years with Abū Ibrāhim ibn Badrān, one of the school's authorized muftis. Towards the end of my reading, he recommended I teach and transmit what I had studied. Following his recommendation, I began presenting Hanbali fiqh online and translating *Zād al-Mustaqniʿ*. I completed the translation of *Zād,* and then added annotations up through the chapter on trade. But my work was never mature enough to publish.

A decade has passed and I feel it is time to carry out my sheikh's recommendation. Instead of reviving a project dormant for a decade, I thought it better to translate a smaller text. So, at the end of December 2015, I started on *Akhṣar al-Mukhtaṣarāt*, one of the more popular later introductions to the school.

The author of the text is Muḥammad bin Badr al-Dīn bin ʿAbd al-Ḥaqq bin Balbān al-Ḥanbalī, born in 1006 AH/1597 CE in the Ṣāliḥiyyah region of Damascus. He was known for his knowledge of hadith and fiqh, including mastery of the four schools, his acts of worship, and his abstinence. His books include *Kāfi al-Mubtadī* which he abridged as *Akhṣar al-Mukhtaṣarāt*, *Mukhtaṣar al-Ifādāt fī Rubʿ al-ʿIbādāt maʿ al-Ādāb wa Ziyādāt,* and a short book on the creed of the Salaf abridged from Ibn Ḥamdān al-Ḥanbalī's *Nihāyat al-Mubtadiʾīn.* He was reported to frequently repeat ʿAlī bin Aḥmed al-Zaydī's statement: "Treat voluntary acts as obligations, sins as disbelief, lusts as poison, mixing with people as fire, and food as medicine." He passed away in 1083 AH/1672 CE.

Not wanting to risk another decade passing without publication, I decided to publish the first quarter covering the major acts of worship: purification, prayer, alms, fasting, pilgrimage, and jihad. While reviewing these chapters I added explanatory notes from al-Baʿlī's commentary *Kashf al-Mukhaddarāt* to clarify the basic text, provide examples, and clarify categorical rulings.

I relied on Dār al-Bashā'ir al-Islāmiyyah's editions of these two books, both edited by Muḥammad Nāsir al-ʿAjmiy. Material from *Kashf* is placed between ‹…›. I kept my own additions to a minimum, placing them between [...].

It is my hope that this translation – along with its future installments – serves English-speaking audiences as an introduction to the basic topics within the Ḥanbalī school. Students will benefit most if they read it with a qualified instructor, perhaps after reading Joe Bradford's *Al-Qaddumi's Elementary Primer in Hanbali Fiqh*.

Those who helped with this project are too numerous to mention. I am ever in debt to Sheikh Abū Ibrāhīm and it has been a great honor to study and sit with him. Many thanks are owed to the Abdul Wahhab and Abdel-Jellal for convincing me to translate a Hanbali text, and to the individuals who reviewed drafts of the translation and offered corrections, encouragement, and advice – especially Anaz Zubair, Annisa Rochadiat, Joe Bradford, and Dropkick Copy's Nabeel Azeez. Many thanks to Nuh and Sumayah for the cover. Last but not least, I owe much to my wife for her constant support and sacrifice over the years.

May Allah grant all who have been mentioned in this preface – and us – His mercy, and may He make us among those who benefit from this text. Where I have succeeded, it is only through the grace of Allah; where I have faltered it is from my own shortcomings.

MUSA FURBER
ABU DHABI
APRIL 20, 2016

PREFACE

This page left blank.

This page left blank.

INTRODUCTION
اَلْمُقَدِّمَةُ

بِسْمِ اَللَّهِ اَلرَّحْمَنِ اَلرَّحِيمِ

In the name of Allah, the Merciful and Compassionate

اَلْحَمْدُ لِلَّهِ اَلْمُفَقِّهِ مَنْ شَاءَ مِنْ خَلْقِهِ فِي اَلدِّينِ، وَالصَّلَاةُ وَالسَّلَامُ عَلَى نَبِيِّنَا مُحَمَّدٍ اَلْأَمِينِ اَلْمُؤَيَّدِ بِكِتَابِهِ اَلْمُبِينِ، اَلْمُتَمَسِّكِ بِحَبْلِهِ اَلْمَتِينِ وَعَلَى أَهْلِهِ وَصَحْبِهِ أَجْمَعِينَ.

All praise belongs to Allah, who gives a deep understanding of religion to whomever of His creation He so wishes. May prayers and greetings be upon our Prophet Muḥammad, the trustworthy one who was strengthened with His clear Book, who held fast to His strong rope ‹i.e., Islam or the Quran›, and upon his Household and all of his Companions.

وَبَعْدُ:

فَقَدْ سَنَحَ بِخَلَدِي أَنْ أَخْتَصِرَ كِتَابِي اَلْمُسَمَّى بِـ«كَافِي اَلْمُبْتَدِي» اَلْكَائِنَ فِي فِقْهِ اَلْإِمَامِ أَحْمَدَ بْنِ حَنْبَلٍ اَلصَّابِرِ لِحُكْمِ اَلْمَلِكِ اَلْمُبْدِي؛ لِيَقْرُبَ تَنَاوُلُهُ عَلَى اَلْمُبْتَدِئِينَ، وَيَسْهُلَ حِفْظُهُ عَلَى اَلرَّاغِبِينَ، وَيَقِلَّ حَجْمُهُ عَلَى اَلطَّالِبِينَ، وَسَمَّيْتُهُ «أَخْصَرَ اَلْمُخْتَصَرَاتِ»؛ لِأَنِّي لَمْ أَقِفْ عَلَى أَخْصَرَ مِنْهُ جَامِعٍ لِمَسَائِلِهِ فِي فِقْهِنَا مِنَ اَلْمُؤَلَّفَاتِ، وَاَللَّهَ أَسْأَلُ أَنْ يَنْفَعَ قَارِئَيْهِ وَحَافِظِيهِ وَنَاظِرِيهِ إِنَّهُ جَدِيرٌ بِإِجَابَةِ اَلدَّعَوَاتِ، وَأَنْ يَجْعَلَهُ خَالِصًا

لِوَجْهِهِ ٱلْكَرِيمِ، مُقَرِّبًا إِلَيْهِ فِي جَنَّاتِ ٱلنَّعِيمِ، وَمَا تَوْفِيقِي [وَاعْتِصَامِي] إِلَّا بِٱللهِ، عَلَيْهِ تَوَكَّلْتُ وَإِلَيْهِ أُنِيبُ.

To commence:

It crossed my mind to abridge my book titled *"Kāfi al-Mubtadī"* (*"The Novice's Sufficiency"*) on the fiqh of Imām Aḥmed bin Ḥanbal (the one who was patient in [following] the Originator's judgment ‹during persecution›) to bring it within reach of novices, facilitate its memorization for desirers, and reduce its bulk for seekers. I named it *"Akhṣar al-Mukhtaṣarāt"* (*"The Most Abridged Abridgment"*) since I have not encountered a shorter Ḥanbalī text amassing its topics. I ask Allah to make it benefit anyone who reads it, memorizes, or ponders it. For indeed, He does answer supplications. And [I ask Allah] to make it purely for His noble sake, to draw closer to Him in the luxurious gardens [of Paradise]. My success and protection are through Allah alone. I rely upon and return to Him.

I

PURIFICATION

كِتَابُ الطَّهَارَةِ

Categories of Water

اَلْمِيَاهُ ثَلَاثَةٌ.

There are three ‹categories› of water.

اَلْأَوَّلُ: طَهُورٌ، وَهُوَ اَلْبَاقِي عَلَى خِلْقَتِهِ وَمِنْهُ مَكْرُوهٌ كَمُتَغَيِّرٍ بِغَيْرِ مُمَازِجٍ وَمُحَرَّمٌ لَا يَرْفَعُ اَلْحَدَثَ وَيُزِيلُ اَلْخَبَثَ، وَهُوَ اَلْمَغْصُوبُ وَغَيْرُ بِئْرِ النَّاقَةِ مِنْ ثَمُودَ.

The first ‹category› is purifying. It is water that remains as it was created.

It includes ‹a type that is› offensive, such as what has changed due to mixing with a non-soluble substance ‹e.g., camphor or grease. This category also includes water changed by sea salt›.

It includes ‹a type that is› unlawful, and does not lift [an individual's state of] impurity yet removes filth.[1] It is stolen water ‹or exchanged for something unlawful›, and water from the lands of Thamūd – except from the well of the camel [of Ṣāliḥ (peace be upon him)].

اَلثَّانِي: طَاهِرٌ لَا يَرْفَعُ اَلْحَدَثَ، وَلَا يُزِيلُ اَلْخَبَثَ، وَهُوَ اَلْمُتَغَيِّرُ بِمُمَازِجٍ طَاهِرٍ وَمِنْهُ يَسِيرٌ مُسْتَعْمَلٌ فِي رَفْعِ حَدَثٍ.

---

1. The author consistently uses "lift" [*yarfaʿ*] with ritual impurity and "remove" [*yuzīl*] with filth. I have maintained this in the translation.

The second ‹category of water› is pure. It does not lift [an individual's state of] ritual impurity or remove filth. It is water that has been changed by mixing with a soluble, pure substance ‹e.g., saffron, milk, honey, and similar pure substances›.

It includes small amounts of water used to lift ritual impurity.

اَلثَّالِثُ: نَجِسٌ يَحْرُمُ اِسْتِعْمَالُهُ مُطْلَقًا، وَهُوَ مَا تَغَيَّرَ بِنَجَاسَةٍ فِي غَيْرِ مَحَلِّ تَطْهِيرٍ أَوْ لَاقَاهَا فِي غَيْرِهِ وَهُوَ يَسِيرٌ، وَالْجَارِي كَالرَّاكِدِ وَالْكَثِيرُ قُلَّتَانِ، وَهُمَا مِائَةُ رِطْلٍ وَسَبْعَةُ أَرْطَالٍ وَسُبْعُ رِطْلٍ بِالدِّمَشْقِيِّ، وَالْيَسِيرُ مَا دُونَهُمَا.

The third ‹category› is filthy. It is categorically [*muṭlaqan*] impermissible to use ‹in acts or worship or otherwise›. It is water changed ‹even slightly› by filth not located in the place being purified or water that has encountered filth elsewhere while being a small quantity. Flowing water is akin to stagnant.

A large quantity ‹of water› is two *qullah*s, which equal 107 1/7 Damascene *riṭl*s [162 liters, 42.8 gallons[2]]. A small quantity of water is less than this.

Containers and Animals

كُلُّ إِنَاءٍ طَاهِرٍ يُبَاحُ اتِّخَاذُهُ وَاسْتِعْمَالُهُ إِلَّا أَنْ يَكُونَ ذَهَبًا، أَوْ فِضَّةً أَوْ مُضَبَّبًا بِأَحَدِهِمَا، لَكِنْ تُبَاحُ ضَبَّةٌ يَسِيرَةٌ مِنْ فِضَّةٍ لِحَاجَةٍ وَمَا لَمْ تُعْلَمْ نَجَاسَتُهُ مِنْ آنِيَةِ كُفَّارٍ، وَثِيَابُهُمْ طَاهِرَةٌ، وَلَا يَطْهُرُ جِلْدُ مَيْتَةٍ بِدِبَاغٍ وَكُلُّ أَجْزَائِهَا نَجِسَةٌ إِلَّا شَعْرًا وَنَحْوَهُ وَالْمُنْفَصِلُ مِنْ حَيٍّ كَمَيْتَتِهِ.

Every container is permissible to acquire and use unless it is [made of] gold or silver, or soldered with either. However, a small amount of silver solder is permissible when needed.

The containers and clothes of non-Muslims are [presumed] pure so long as an item is not known to be filthy.

---

2. See Ibn Jāmiʿ, *Al-Fawāʾid al-Muntakhabāt,* 1:22.

The skin of an unslaughtered animal ‹that became filthy by dying› is not purified via tanning. All of its parts are filth, except its hair and the like ‹e.g., feathers and wool; as these remain pure when they are from an animal that is pure while alive, or an inedible animal like a cat or something smaller.›

Anything separated from a live creature is akin to an unslaughtered creature of its type ‹in being pure or filthy›.

Going to the Lavatory

(فَصْلٌ) اَلِاسْتِنْجَاءُ وَاجِبٌ مِنْ كُلِّ خَارِجٍ إِلَّا اَلرِّيحَ وَالطَّاهِرَ وَغَيْرَ اَلْمُلَوِّثِ

Cleaning oneself with water or stones or their like [*istinjā*ʾ] is obligatory for everything exiting [the waste passages] ‹whether rare (like worms) or common (like urine)› – except flatulence, pure substances, and whatever does not defile ‹e.g., kidney stones›.

وَسُنَّ عِنْدَ دُخُولِ خَلَاءٍ قَوْلُ: «بِسْمِ اَللهِ اَللَّهُمَّ إِنِّي أَعُوذُ بِكَ مِنَ اَلْخُبُثِ وَالْخَبَائِثِ» وَبَعْدَ خُرُوجٍ مِنْهُ: «غُفْرَانَكَ» «اَلْحَمْدُ للهِ اَلَّذِي أَذْهَبَ عَنِّي اَلْأَذَى وَعَافَانِي»، وَتَغْطِيَةُ رَأْسٍ وَانْتِعَالٌ، وَتَقْدِيمُ رِجْلِهِ اَلْيُسْرَى دُخُولًا، وَاعْتِمَادُهُ عَلَيْهَا جُلُوسًا، وَالْيُمْنَى خُرُوجًا، عَكْسُ مَسْجِدٍ وَنَعْلٍ وَنَحْوِهِمَا، وَبُعْدٌ فِي فَضَاءٍ، وَطَلَبُ مَكَانٍ رَخْوٍ لِبَوْلٍ، وَمَسْحُ اَلذَّكَرِ بِالْيَدِ اَلْيُسْرَى إِذَا اِنْقَطَعَ اَلْبَوْلُ مِنْ أَصْلِهِ إِلَى رَأْسِهِ ثَلَاثًا، وَنَتْرُهُ ثَلَاثًا.

It is recommended to say when entering the lavatory

> "*Bismi Llāh, Allāhumma innī aʿūdhu bika mina l-khubthi wa l-khabāʾith*"
>
> ("In the name of Allah. O Allah, verily I seek protection through You from male and female devils.")

and when exiting

> "*Ghufrānak al-ḥamdu Lillāhi lladhi adhhaba ʿannī al-adhā wa ʿāfānī*"
>
> ("Grant me Your forgiveness. Praise belongs to Allah, who removed harm from me and cured me").

[When going to the lavatory] ‹it is recommended› to cover the head; to wear sandals; to step in with one's left and favor it when sitting; to exit with the right (opposite to the mosque, sandals, and the like ‹e.g., entering schools and wearing clothes›); to distance oneself in vacant areas; to seek soft ground for urination; to wipe the penis with the left hand after urinating, from base to tip three times; and to tap it three times.

وَكُرِهَ دُخُولُ خَلَاءٍ بِمَا فِيهِ ذِكْرُ اللهِ -تَعَالَى- وَكَلَامٌ فِيهِ بِلَا حَاجَةٍ، وَرَفْعُ ثَوْبٍ قَبْلَ دُنُوٍّ مِنَ الْأَرْضِ، وَبَوْلٌ فِي شَقٍّ وَنَحْوِهِ، وَمَسُّ فَرْجٍ بِيَمِينٍ بِلَا حَاجَةٍ، وَاسْتِقْبَالُ النَّيِّرَيْنِ وَحَرُمَ اسْتِقْبَالُ قِبْلَةٍ وَاسْتِدْبَارُهَا فِي غَيْرِ بُنْيَانٍ، وَلُبْثٌ فَوْقَ الْحَاجَةِ، وَبَوْلٌ فِي طَرِيقٍ مَسْلُوكٍ وَنَحْوِهِ وَتَحْتَ شَجَرَةٍ مُثْمِرَةٍ ثَمَرًا مَقْصُودًا.

It is offensive to enter the lavatory with anything bearing mention of Allah Most High; to speak therein without need; to lift one's garment before drawing close to the ground; to urinate in crevices and the like ‹e.g., holes, burrows and dens›; to touch one's penis with the right hand without need; to face the sun or the moon it being unlawful to face or turn one's back to the direction of prayer when not in [or between] buildings; to remain longer than needed; to urinate in a trodden path or the like ‹e.g., shaded areas in summer, sunny areas in winter, places where people congregate for permissible conversation›; and to urinate under a fruit-bearing tree with fruit that is sought ‹whether or not they are eaten›.

وَسُنَّ اسْتِجْمَارٌ ثُمَّ اسْتِنْجَاءٌ بِمَاءٍ، وَيَجُوزُ الِاقْتِصَارُ عَلَى أَحَدِهِمَا، لَكِنَّ الْمَاءَ أَفْضَلُ حِينَئِذٍ، وَلَا يَصِحُّ اسْتِجْمَارٌ إِلَّا بِطَاهِرٍ مُبَاحٍ يَابِسٍ مُنَقٍّ وَحَرُمَ

بِرَوْثٍ وَعَظْمٍ وَطَعَامٍ وَذِي حُرْمَةٍ وَمُتَّصِلٍ بِحَيَوَانٍ، وَشُرِطَ لَهُ عَدَمُ تَعَدِّي خَارِجٍ مَوْضِعَ ٱلْعَادَةِ وَثَلَاثُ مَسَحَاتٍ مُنَقِّيَةٍ فَأَكْثَرُ.

It is recommended to clean oneself via *istijmār* ‹with stones and their like› and then with water. ‹The opposite order is offensive.› It is permissible to limit oneself to one of them though in that case water is superior.

It is not permissible to clean oneself via *istijmār* except by something pure, permissible to use, dry, and capable of cleaning the area.

It is not permissible to clean oneself with dung, bones, food ‹even animal food›, anything possessing sanctity ‹e.g., books containing beneficial knowledge›, or part of an animal when it is attached to the animal.

A condition for cleaning via *istijmār* is that the filth does not move beyond its typical location and that there be at least three clean wipes.

The Toothstick and Other Sunnahs of the Body

(فَصْلٌ) يَسُنُّ ٱلسِّوَاكُ بِالْعُودِ كُلَّ وَقْتٍ، إِلَّا لِصَائِمٍ بَعْدَ ٱلزَّوَالِ فَيُكْرَهُ. وَيَتَأَكَّدُ عِنْدَ صَلَاةٍ وَنَحْوِهَا وَتَغَيُّرِ فَمٍ وَنَحْوِهِ.

Using toothsticks is recommended at all times except after the sun has reached its zenith for someone who is fasting – for that is offensive. Its usage is emphasized at prayer and the like ‹e.g., for ablution, reciting Quran, entering the mosque or one's house›, when the mouth changes and the like ‹e.g., after sleep, lengthy periods of silence, yellowing of the teeth, and an empty stomach›.

وَسُنَّ بُدَاءَةٌ بِالْأَيْمَنِ فِيهِ، وَفِي طُهْرٍ وَشَأْنِهِ كُلِّهِ، وَادِّهَانٌ غِبًّا، وَاكْتِحَالٌ فِي كُلِّ عَيْنٍ ثَلَاثًا، وَنَظَرٌ فِي مِرْآةٍ، وَتَطَيُّبٌ، وَاسْتِحْدَادٌ وَحَفُّ شَارِبٍ وَتَقْلِيمُ ظُفُرٍ، وَنَتْفُ إِبِطٍ وَكُرِهَ قَزَعٌ وَنَتْفُ شَيْبٍ، وَثَقْبُ أُذُنِ صَبِيٍّ، وَيَجِبُ خِتَانُ ذَكَرٍ وَأُنْثَى بُعَيْدَ بُلُوغٍ مَعَ أَمِنِ ٱلضَّرَرِ، وَيُسَنُّ قَبْلَهُ، وَيُكْرَهُ سَابِعَ وِلَادَتِهِ وَمِنْهَا إِلَيْهِ.

It is recommended to begin with the right side of the mouth when using it.

‹Beginning with the right is also recommended› during purification and in all of one's affairs.

‹It is recommended› to apply oil every other day; to apply *kohl* to each eye three times ‹nightly›; to look in the mirror; to use perfume; remove pubic hair; to crop one's mustache; to pare one's nails; and to pluck armpit hair.

It is offensive to shave part of the head; to pluck white hairs; or to pierce a young boy's ears.

It is obligatory to circumcise males ‹by removing the foreskin› and females ‹by removing the skin above the vagina resembling a cock's crest [i.e., the clitoral hood]. It is recommended not to take all of it.›[3] soon after reaching maturity when there is safety from harm. It is recommended to do so before maturity. It is offensive to do so from birth up to and including the seventh day.

Obligatory and Recommended Acts of Ablution

(فَصْلٌ) فُرُوضُ اَلْوُضُوءِ سِتَّةٌ: غَسْلُ اَلْوَجْهِ مَعَ مَضْمَضَةٍ وَاسْتِنْشَاقٍ، وَغَسْلُ اَلْيَدَيْنِ، وَالرِّجْلَيْنِ وَمَسْحُ جَمِيعِ اَلرَّأْسِ مَعَ اَلْأُذُنَيْنِ، وَتَرْتِيبٌ وَمُوَالَاةٌ.

The obligatory acts of ablution are six:

‹1› washing the face including rinsing the mouth and nostrils;
‹2–3› washing the arms and feet ‹including the elbows and ankles›;
‹4› wiping all of the head including the ears;
‹5› ordering ‹the limbs as Allah Most High mentioned them›; and,
‹6› consecutiveness.

‹The [last] two are dropped when making the purificatory bath for major impurity.›

3. There is an opinion within the school that it is not required for women. This opinion was preferred by many Hanbali scholars, including Ibn Qudāmah. See Ibn Qudāmah, *Al-Mughnī,* 1:64; and ʿAlī al-Mardāwī, *Al-Inṣāf,* 1:124.

وَالنِّيَّةُ شَرْطٌ لِكُلِّ طَهَارَةٍ شَرْعِيَّةٍ غَيْرَ إِزَالَةِ خَبَثٍ، وَغُسْلِ كِتَابِيَّةٍ لِحِلِّ وَطْءٍ وَمُسْلِمَةٍ مُمْتَنِعَةٍ.

The intention is a condition for every legal act of purification except for removing filth, a non-Muslim female performing the purificatory bath ‹for menstruation, lochia, and the like› to render intercourse permissible, and a Muslim female who refuses ‹[to perform the bath] for the same [reasons]›.

‹The conditions for ablution are eight: conclusion of the act that obligates it; the intention; being Muslim; sanity; discernment; pure and lawful water; removing whatever prevents it from reaching the body; and having cleaned oneself of filth [*istinjāʾ*].›

وَالتَّسْمِيَةُ وَاجِبَةٌ فِي وُضُوءٍ وَغُسْلٍ وَتَيَمُّمٍ وَغَسْلِ يَدَيْ قَائِمٍ مِنْ نَوْمِ لَيْلٍ نَاقِضٍ لِوُضُوءٍ وَتَسْقُطُ سَهْوًا وَجَهْلاً.

Saying "*bismi Llāh*" is an obligation ‹in five places›: during ablution, the purificatory bath, dry ablution, and someone washing their hands after waking from sleep that invalidated their ablution. ‹The fifth is when washing the deceased.› The obligation ceases due to forgetfulness and ignorance.

وَمِنْ سُنَنِهِ اسْتِقْبَالُ قِبْلَةٍ، وَسِوَاكٌ، وَبُدَاءَةٌ بِغَسْلِ يَدَي غَيْرِ قَائِمٍ مِنْ نَوْمِ لَيْلٍ، وَيَجِبُ لَهُ ثَلَاثًا تَعَبُّدًا، وَبِمَضْمَضَةٍ فَاسْتِنْشَاقٍ وَمُبَالَغَةٌ فِيهِمَا لِغَيْرِ صَائِمٍ، وَتَخْلِيلُ شَعْرٍ كَثِيفٍ وَالْأَصَابِعِ [وغَسْلَةٌ] ثَانِيَةٌ وَثَالِثَةٌ، وَكُرِهَ أَكْثَرُ.

وَسُنَّ بَعْدَ فَرَاغِهِ رَفْعُ بَصَرِهِ إِلَى اَلسَّمَاءِ وَقَوْلُ مَا وَرَدَ وَاللهُ أَعْلَمُ.

Its recommended acts include: facing the direction of prayer [*qiblah*]; using the toothstick [*miswāk*]; starting by washing the hands (for someone who is not rising from having slept at night, as such a person must wash them three times, out of being devotional [*taʿbbudan*]); rinsing the mouth before the nostrils, and to do so vigorously if one is not fasting; combing one's fingers through thick hair, and between one's fingers and toes; performing a second and third washing – more than this is offensive.

It is recommended after finishing ablution to raise one's gaze to the sky and to say what has been transmitted

> ‹"*Ashhadu an lā ilāha illa Llāhu waḥdahu lā sharīka lahu, wa ashhadu anna Muḥammadan ʿabduhu wa rasūluhu, Allāhumma jʿalnī mina t-tawwābīn wa jʿalnī mina l-mutaṭahhirīn, subḥānaka Allāumma wa bi ḥamdika, ashhadu an lā ilāha illā anta, astaghfiruka wa atūbu ilayk*"
>
> ("I testify that there is no deity other than Allah, alone and without partner. And I testify that Muḥammad [ﷺ] is His servant and His messenger. O Allah, make me amongst the penitent and the purified. Glory is Yours, O Allah, and through Your praise. I testify that there is no deity other than You. I seek Your forgiveness and repent to You.")›.

And Allah knows best.

Wiping over Footgear

(فَصْلٌ) يَجُوزُ ٱلْمَسْحُ عَلَى خُفٍّ وَنَحْوِهِ وَعِمَامَةِ ذَكَرٍ مُحَنَّكَةٍ أَوْ ذَاتِ ذُؤَابَةٍ، وَخُمُرِ نِسَاءٍ مُدَارَةٍ تَحْتَ حُلُوقِهِنَّ وَعَلَى جَبِيرَةٍ لَمْ تُجَاوِزْ قَدْرَ ٱلْحَاجَةِ إِلَى حَلِّهَا، وَإِنْ جَاوَزَتْهُ أَوْ وَضَعَهَا عَلَى غَيْرِ طَهَارَةٍ لَزِمَ نَزْعُهَا، فَإِنْ خَافَ ٱلضَّرَرَ تَيَمَّمَ، مَعَ مَسْحِ مَوْضُوعَةٍ عَلَى طَهَارَةٍ. وَيَمْسَحُ مُقِيمٌ وَعَاصٍ بِسَفَرِهِ مِنْ حَدَثٍ بَعْدَ لُبْسٍ يَوْمًا وَلَيْلَةً، وَمُسَافِرٌ سَفَرَ قَصْرٍ ثَلَاثَةً بِلَيَالِيهَا.

It is permissible to wipe over leather socks [*khuff*] and their like ‹e.g., layers of leather socks, socks, and other barriers – provided their conditions are met›; a male's turban that wraps under the chin or has a tail [*dhuʾābah*]; and over a woman's head-covering that wraps below the bottom of the mouth.

‹It is permissible to wipe› over bandages that do not exceed the amount needed, until the bandages are removed. If the bandage exceeds the needed area or was wrapped while not having ritual purity, it must be removed. Though if one fears harm from removing it, one makes dry ablution combined with wiping over what was placed while having ritual purity.

The resident or one whose travel is sinful wipes for one day and night, starting from the time their ablution was invalidated after wearing [the *khuff* or a similar barrier]. A traveler who shortens prayers wipes for three days and nights.

فَإِنْ مَسَحَ فِي سَفَرٍ ثُمَّ أَقَامَ أَوْ عَكَسَ فَكَمُقِيمٍ،

وَشُرِطَ تَقَدُّمُ كَمَالِ طَهَارَةٍ وَسَتْرُ مَمْسُوحٍ مَحَلَّ فَرْضٍ وَثُبُوتُهُ بِنَفْسِهِ، وَإِمْكَانُ مَشْيٍ بِهِ عُرْفًا وَطَهَارَتُهُ وَإِبَاحَتُهُ.

If one wipes while traveling and then becomes a resident (or the opposite), he is akin to a resident [so he wipes for up to one day and night].

Stipulated ‹for wiping over *khuff* and similar barriers› are ‹seven conditions›:

‹1› to have a complete purification ‹using water›;

‹2› that the wiped barrier covers the area obligatory [*farḍ*] to wash;

‹3–4› that they attach [to the foot] on their own ‹or by wearing sandals over them›, and can be walked in a manner customarily considered walking;

‹5› that they are pure; and

‹6› that they are permissible for use.

‹A seventh condition is that they do not describe the skin due to being translucent (like thin glass) or thinness (like sheer socks).›

وَيَجِبُ مَسْحُ أَكْثَرِ دَوَائِرِ عِمَامَةٍ، وَأَكْثَرِ ظَاهِرِ قَدَمِ خُفٍّ، وَجَمِيعُ جَبِيرَةٍ، وَإِنْ ظَهَرَ بَعْضُ مَحَلِّ فَرْضٍ أو تَمَّتْ ٱلْمُدَّةُ اسْتَأْنَفَ ٱلطَّهَارَةَ.

It is obligatory to wipe the majority of a turban's loops, the majority of the top of the foot, and the entirety of a bandage. If part of what must [*farḍ*] be washed [during ablution] becomes visible or the duration expires, one recommences ablution.

Ablution Invalidators

(فَصْلٌ) نَوَاقِضُ ٱلْوُضُوءِ ثَمَانِيَةٌ: خَارِجٌ مِنْ سَبِيلٍ مُطْلَقًا وَخَارِجٌ مِنْ بَقِيَّةِ ٱلْبَدَنِ مِنْ بَوْلٍ وَغَائِطٍ وَكَثِيرِ نَجِسٍ غَيْرِهِمْ وَزَوَالُ عَقْلٍ إِلَّا يَسِيرَ نَوْمٍ مِنْ قَائِمٍ أَوْ قَاعِدٍ وَغُسْلُ مَيِّتٍ وَأَكْلُ لَحْمِ إِبِلٍ، وَالرِّدَّةُ، وَكُلُّ مَا أَوْجَبَ غُسْلاً غَيْرَ مَوْتٍ، وَمَسُّ فَرْجِ آدَمِيٍّ مُتَّصِلٍ أَوْ حَلْقَةِ دُبُرِهِ بِيَدٍ، وَلَمْسُ ذَكَرٍ أَوْ أُنْثَى ٱلْآخَرَ لِشَهْوَةٍ بِلَا حَائِلٍ فِيهِمَا، لَا لِشَعْرٍ وَسِنٍّ وَظُفْرٍ وَلَا بِهَا وَلَا مَنْ دُونَ سَبْعٍ.

Eight things invalidate ablution:

‹1› whatever exits from a waste-passage, categorically [*muṭlaqan*] ‹small or large›;

‹2› urine or feces, or a large amount of other filth ‹like vomit, blood, and puss› exiting from the rest of the body;

‹3› loss of consciousness – except for light dozing from someone standing or seated;

‹4› washing a deceased;

‹5› eating camel meat;

‹6› apostasy and everything that requires taking the purificatory bath except death;

‹7› touching the unsevered front private parts or the anus of a human being with one's hand ‹including the palm, back of the hands, or the edges of the fingers or hand›; and,

‹8› touching someone of the opposite sex with arousal without a barrier. But ‹touching does› not ‹invalidate ablution› when the part touched or doing the touching is the hair or tooth or nail, nor when it involves someone less than seven years old.

وَلَا يَنْتَقِضُ وُضُوءُ مَلْمُوسٍ مُطْلَقًا، وَمَنْ شَكَّ فِي طَهَارَةٍ أَوْ حَدَثٍ بَنَى عَلَى يَقِينِهِ.

The ablution of the person touched is never invalidated, categorically [*muṭlaqan*] ‹regardless of arousal and the ages involved›.

Whoever has doubt about ritual purity ‹after being certain of ritual impurity› and ritual impurity ‹after being certain of ritual purity› bases their actions on their certitude ‹impurity in the former, and purity in the latter›.

وَحَرُمَ عَلَى مُحْدِثٍ مَسُّ مُصْحَفٍ وَصَلَاةٌ وَطَوَافٌ، وَعَلَى جُنُبٍ وَنَحْوِهِ ذَلِكَ، وَقِرَاءَةُ آيَةِ قُرْآنٍ، وَلُبْثٌ فِي مَسْجِدٍ بِغَيْرِ وُضُوءٍ.

It is unlawful for someone in the state of minor ritual impurity to touch the printed Quran [*muṣḥaf*], pray, or perform circumambulation.

[It is unlawful] for someone in the state of sexual pollution [*janābah*] and the like ‹e.g., [after the end of] menstruation and lochia› to do the same, recite a verse of the Quran, or remain in a mosque without ablution.

Occasions Obligating the Purificatory Bath

(فَصْلٌ) مُوجِبَاتُ ٱلْغُسْلِ سَبْعَةٌ: خُرُوجُ ٱلْمَنِيِّ مِنْ مَخْرَجِهِ بِلَذَّةٍ وَانْتِقَالُهُ وَتَغْيِيبُ حَشَفَةٍ فِي فَرْجٍ أَوْ دُبُرٍ وَلَوْ لِبَهِيمَةٍ أَوْ مَيِّتٍ بِلَا حَائِلٍ، وَإِسْلَامُ كَافِرٍ، وَمَوْتٌ، وَحَيْضٌ، وَنِفَاسٌ.

Seven occasions obligate the purificatory bath:

‹1–2› the exit of fluid typically released during orgasm [*manī*] from its orifice with pleasure; and its moving ‹from its source, even if it does not exit›;

‹3› the insertion of the glans of the penis into a vagina or anus – even into an animal or a dead being – without a barrier;

‹4› a non-Muslim entering Islam;

‹5› death;
‹6› menstruation; and,
‹7› lochia.

وَسُنَّ لِجُمُعَةٍ، وَعِيدٍ، وَكُسُوفٍ، وَاسْتِسْقَاءٍ وَجُنُونٍ، وَإِغْمَاءٍ لَا احْتِلَامَ فِيهِمَا، وَاسْتِحَاضَةٍ لِكُلِّ صَلَاةٍ، وَإِحْرَامٍ، وَدُخُولِ مَكَّةَ، وَحَرَمِهَا، وَوُقُوفٍ بِعَرَفَةَ، وَطَوَافِ زِيَارَةٍ، وَوَدَاعٍ، وَمَبِيتٍ بِمُزْدَلِفَةَ، ورَمْيِ جمارٍ.

‹The purificatory bath› is recommended for ‹sixteen occasions›:
‹1–5› the Friday Prayer, ‹for washing the deceased,› Eid, Eclipse, and Drought [Prayers];
‹6› insanity;
‹7› loss of consciousness unaccompanied by ejaculation;
‹8› irregular vaginal bleeding (for each prayer);
‹9› entering the state of pilgrimage [*iḥrām*];
‹10–11› entering Mecca and its Sanctuary;
‹12› standing on ʿArafah;
‹13–14› the Visitation and Farewell Circumambulations;
‹15› staying the night at Muzdalifah; and,
‹16› throwing [stones] at [the three] pillars.

وَتَنْقُضُ الْمَرْأَةُ شَعْرَهَا لِحَيْضٍ وَنِفَاسٍ، لَا جَنَابَةٍ إِذَا رَوَتْ أُصُولَهُ.

A woman undoes her braids [when bathing] due to menstruation and lochia – but not [when washing] for sexual pollution [*janābah*] when the water reaches the roots.

وَسُنَّ تَوَضُّؤٌ بِمُدٍّ، وَاغْتِسَالٌ بِصَاعٍ وَكُرِهَ إِسْرَافٌ وَإِنْ نَوَى بِالْغُسْلِ رَفْعَ الْحَدَثَيْنِ أَوْ الْحَدَثِ وَأَطْلَقَ ارْتَفَعَا.

It is recommended to use one *mudd* [0.51 liters] of water for ablution, and one *ṣāʿ* [2.04 liters] for the purificatory bath. It is offensive to waste water.

If one's intention for the purificatory bath is to lift the state of both minor and major ritual impurity, or to lift impurity without restriction, both are lifted.

وَسُنَّ لِجُنُبٍ غَسْلُ فَرْجِهِ، وَالْوُضُوءُ لِأَكْلٍ وَشُرْبٍ وَنَوْمٍ، وَمُعَاوَدَةِ وَطْءٍ، وَالْغُسْلُ لَهَا أَفْضَلُ، وَكُرِهَ نَوْمُ جُنُبٍ بِلَا وُضُوءٍ.

It is recommended for someone in a state of sexual pollution [*janābah*] to wash their genitals, and to make ablution for eating, drinking, sleeping, or repeating intercourse. It is better to perform the purificatory bath for these. It is offensive for someone in a state of sexual pollution [*janābah*] to sleep without making ablution.

Dry Ablution

(فَصْلٌ) يَصِحُّ اَلتَّيَمُّمُ بِتُرَابٍ طَهُورٍ مُبَاحٍ لَهُ غُبَارٌ إِذَا عُدِمَ اَلْمَاءُ لِحَبْسٍ أَوْ غَيْرِهِ، أَوْ خِيفَ بِاسْتِعْمَالِهِ، أَوْ طَلَبِهِ ضَرَرٌ بِبَدَنٍ أَوْ مَالٍ أَوْ غَيْرِهِمَا، وَيُفْعَلُ عَنْ كُلِّ مَا يُفْعَلُ بِالْمَاءِ سِوَى نَجَاسَةٍ عَلَى غَيْرِ بَدَنٍ إِذَا دَخَلَ وَقْتُ فَرْضٍ وَأُبِيحَ غَيْرُهُ.

Dry ablution is valid with ‹eight conditions›:

‹1–5 the intention; being a Muslim who is sane, has discernment, and having cleaned oneself of filth via stones or water;›

‹6› using purifying earth that is permissible [to the user] and contains dirt;

‹7› the absence of water due to confinement ‹of the water from him, or him from the water› or the like ‹e.g., enemies cutting off their water, or not able to draw water from the well›; or due to fear that using or seeking water will be harmful to his life, property, or another ‹e.g., human or animal, or it being needed for cooking, or it being sold far above its typical price›; and,

‹8› when the time of an obligatory [*farḍ*] prayer has entered or a non-obligatory prayer is permissible.

It ‹dry ablution› is performed for everything done with water – except for non-bodily filth [e.g. on the clothes].[4]

---

4. In the original text, this line comes before the one above it. It has been moved here to keep the conditions together.

وَإِنْ وَجَدَ مَاءً لَا يَكْفِي طَهَارَتَهُ اِسْتَعْمَلَهُ ثُمَّ تَيَمَّمَ.

If one found water but it is not sufficient for purification, one uses it [for ablution] and then makes dry ablution.

وَيَتَيَمَّمُ لِلْجُرْحِ عِنْدَ غَسْلِهِ، إِنْ لَمْ يُمْكِنْ مَسْحُهُ بِالْمَاءِ وَيَغْسِلُ اَلصَّحِيحَ.

One makes dry ablution for a wound when one would wash it if it is not possible to wipe it with water, and [one] washes the healthy [parts].[5]

‹One who has a wound on some of the limbs of ablution must observe the order for raising minor ritual impurity when making ablution [...]. Consequently, one makes dry ablution for a wound when one would wash it when it is healthy. So if the wound is on the face in a way that he cannot wash any of it, he makes dry ablution first and then completes ablution. If the wound is on part of his face, he chooses between washing the healthy part and then making dry ablution for the wounded part; or making dry ablution, and then washing the healthy part and continuing ablution. If the injury is on another limb, he must wash whatever comes before it and then do as mentioned with the face. If the injury is on his face, hands, and feet, each limb needs a dry ablution where it would [otherwise] be washed in order to preserve the order. If he were to wash the healthy part of his face and then make a single dry ablution for it and his hands, it would not suffice [...].

[The above applies] if it is not possible to wipe the injury with water.

If it is possible to wipe the injury with water, it is obligatory and suffices since washing is commanded and wiping is included – just like someone who is unable to bow and prostrate but is able to nod must nod. [In such a case, one also] washes the healthy [portion of the limb].

5. For the sake of clarity, the basic text has been presented first without commentary. The following paragraphs present the basic text grouped together with its commentary grouped separately and edited slightly to increase clarity.

One who has a wound on some of the limbs of ablution is also required when making ablution to observe consecutiveness when lifting minor ritual impurity, so he is required to wash the healthy [portion of the limb] with every dry ablution.›

وَطَلَبُ اَلْمَاءِ شَرْطٌ فَإِنْ نَسِيَ قُدْرَتَهُ عَلَيْهِ وَتَيَمَّمَ أَعَادَ.

Seeking water is a condition. If he forgot that he can obtain water ‹such as forgetting that one can buy it or has enough to purchase it› and made dry ablution, he must repeat [whatever he prayed].

وَفُرُوضُهُ: مَسْحُ وَجْهِهِ، وَيَدَيْهِ إِلَىَّ كُوعَيْهِ، وَفِي أَصْغَرَ تَرْتِيبٌ وَمُوَالَاةٌ أَيْضًا.

Its obligatory actions are ‹four›:
‹1–2› wiping the face and the hands up to the wrists; and,
‹3–4› when performing dry ablution for minor ritual impurity ‹i.e., in place of minor impurity›, its order and consecutiveness are also obligatory.

وَنِيَّةُ اَلِاسْتِبَاحَةِ شَرْطٌ لِمَا يَتَيَمَّمُ لَهُ، وَلَا يُصَلِّي بِهِ فَرْضًا، إِنْ نَوَى نَفْلًا أَوْ أَطْلَقَ.

Intending making an action licit [al-istibāḥah] is a condition for whatever dry ablution is performed for ‹i.e. minor or major ritual impurity, or for filth on the body›. One does not pray an obligatory [farḍ] prayer if one intended a voluntary prayer or did not specify [aṭlaqa].

وَيَبْطُلُ بِخُرُوجِ اَلْوَقْتِ، وَمُبْطِلَاتِ اَلْوُضُوءِ، وَبِوُجُودِ مَاءٍ إِنْ تَيَمَّمَ لِفَقْدِهِ. وَسُنَّ لِرَاجِيهِ تَأْخِيرٌ لِآخِرِ وَقْتٍ مُخْتَارٍ.

Dry ablution is invalidated ‹by five:›
‹1› when the time [of the current prayer] has elapsed;
‹2 conclusion of whatever makes it permissible – such as when one makes dry ablution for a sickness and then recovers, or for cold that ends;›

‹3 removing what is wiped over;›
‹4› whatever invalidates ablution; and,
‹5› the presence of water if performed for its absence. It is recommended for someone expecting water to wait until the end of a prayer's preferred time of performance.

وَمَنْ عَدِمَ ٱلْمَاءَ وَالتُّرَابَ أَوْ لَمْ يُمْكِنْهُ اِسْتِعْمَالُهُمَا صَلَّى ٱلْفَرْضَ فَقَطْ عَلَى حَسَبِ حَالِهِ،
وَلَا إِعَادَةَ، وَيَقْتَصِرُ عَلَى مُجْزِئٍ، وَلَا يَقْرَأُ فِي غَيْرِ ٱلصَّلَاةِ إِنْ كَانَ جُنُبًا.

Whoever lacks water and earth or is not able to use them prays just the obligatory [*farḍ*] prayer however his conditions allow. He is not required to repeat [these prayers]. He limits himself to what suffices and does not recite [Quran] outside of prayer if he has sexual pollution [*janābah*] ‹or anything else that requires the purificatory bath›.

Cleaning and Removing Filth

(فَصْلٌ) تَطْهُرُ أَرْضٌ وَنَحْوُهَا بِإِزَالَةِ عَيْنِ ٱلنَّجَاسَةِ وَأَثَرِهَا بِالْمَاءِ، وَبَوْلُ غُلَامٍ لَمْ
يَأْكُلْ طَعَامًا بِشَهْوَةٍ، وَقَيْئُهُ يَغْمُرُهُ بِهِ،

The ground and its like ‹e.g., rocks, walls› are purified by removing the filthy substance and its traces with water.
The urine and vomit of a male infant who has not eaten food desirously [are purified] by dousing it ‹with water›.

وَغَيْرُهُمَا بِسَبْعِ غَسَلَاتٍ، أَحَدُهَا بِتُرَابٍ وَنَحْوِهِ فِي نَجَاسَةِ كَلْبٍ وَخِنْزِيرٍ فَقَطْ مَعَ
زَوَالِهَا، وَلَا يَضُرُّ بَقَاءُ لَوْنٍ أَوْ رِيحٍ أَوْ هُمَا عَجْزًا

Other types of filth are purified by seven washings – one of which is accompanied by earth or its like ‹e.g., saltwort, bran, soap›, for filth from dogs and pigs ‹but no other animal› – combined with its removal. The color, smell, or both remaining does not harm purification if they cannot be removed. ‹But the taste remaining harms purification since taste indicates that the substance remains.›

وَتَطْهُرُ خَمْرَةٌ اِنْقَلَبَتْ بِنَفْسِهَا خَلًّا، وَكَذَا دَنُّهَا لَا دُهْنٌ وَمُتَشَرِّبُ نَجَاسَةً.

Any wine that becomes vinegar on its own is pure, as is its container. But oil and something that has absorbed filth ‹like paste› do not ‹become pure›.

وَعُفِيَ فِي غَيْرِ مَائِعٍ وَمَطْعُومٍ عَنْ يَسِيرِ دَمٍ نَجِسٍ وَنَحْوِهِ مِنْ حَيَوَانٍ طَاهِرٍ لَا دَمَ سَبِيلٍ إِلَّا مِنْ حَيْضٍ،

Small amounts of filthy blood and the like ‹e.g., pus› from a pure animal are excusable – except when present in liquids or edibles. But blood from the waste passages is not excusable – except for menstrual blood ‹and lochia and irregular vaginal bleeding›.

وَمَا لَا نَفْسَ لَهُ سَائِلَةٌ، وَقَمْلٌ وَبَرَاغِيثُ وَبَعُوضٌ وَنَحْوُهَا طَاهِرَةٌ مُطْلَقًا

Whatever lacks flowing blood, lice, fleas, mosquitoes, and the like ‹including flies› – categorically [*muṭlaqan*] ‹alive or dead› – are pure.

وَمَائِعٌ مُسْكِرٌ، وَمَا لَا يُؤْكَلُ مِنْ طَيْرٍ وَبَهَائِمَ مِمَّا فَوْقَ اَلْهِرِّ خِلْقَةً، وَلَبَنٌ وَمَنِيٌّ مِنْ غَيْرِ آدَمِيٍّ وَبَوْلٌ وَرَوْثٌ، وَنَحْوُهَا مِنْ غَيْرِ مَأْكُولِ اَللَّحْمِ نَجِسَةٌ، وَمِنْهُ طَاهِرَةٌ كَمِمَّا لَا دَمَ لَهُ سَائِلٌ.

[The following] are filthy: liquid intoxicants; birds and land-animals that are not eaten and which are larger than cats; milk and sperm from non-humans.

[The following] are filthy [when] from an animal whose meat is not eaten: urine, feces, and the like ‹e.g., vomit, pre-ejaculate [*madhī*], prostatic fluid [*wadī*], mucus, saliva›.

They are pure from edible animals, just as they are from animals without flowing blood.

وَيُعْفَى عَنْ يَسِيرِ طِينِ شَارِعٍ عُرْفًا إِنْ عُلِمَتْ نَجَاسَتُهُ وَإِلَّا فَطَاهِرٌ.

Mud on the street typically considered a small amount is excused if known to be filthy. Otherwise, it is pure.

Menstruation

(فَصْلٌ) لَا حَيْضَ مَعَ حَمْلٍ، وَلَا بَعْدَ خَمْسِينَ سَنَةً وَلَا قَبْلَ تَمَامِ تِسْعِ سِنِينَ.

Menstruation does not occur during pregnancy, after fifty ‹lunar› years of age, nor before completing nine ‹lunar› years of age.

وَأَقَلُّهُ يَوْمٌ وَلَيْلَةٌ وَأَكْثَرُهُ خَمْسَةَ عَشَرَ وَغَالِبُهُ سِتٌّ أَوْ سَبْعٌ، وَأَقَلُّ طُهْرٍ بَيْنَ حَيْضَتَيْنِ ثَلَاثَةَ عَشَرَ، وَلَا حَدَّ لِأَكْثَرِهِ، وَحَرُمَ عَلَيْهَا فِعْلُ صَلَاةٍ وَصَوْمٍ، وَيَلْزَمُهَا قَضَاؤُهُ وَيَجِبُ بِوَطْئِهَا فِي الْفَرْجِ دِينَارٌ أَوْ نِصْفُهُ كَفَّارَةً، وَتُبَاحُ الْمُبَاشَرَةُ فِيمَا دُونَهُ.

The minimal duration ‹for menstruation› is a single day and night. The maximum is fifteen days. The norm is six or seven days.

The minimum duration of purity between two menstruations is thirteen days. It has no maximum.

It is unlawful for a woman ‹during menstruation› to perform prayer and to fast. She is required to make up the fast.

One must pay a whole *dīnār* or half a *dīnār* as an expiation for having vaginal intercourse during menstruation. Non-vaginal foreplay is permissible.

وَالْمُبْتَدَأَةُ تَجْلِسُ أَقَلَّهُ ثُمَّ تَغْتَسِلُ وَتُصَلِّي، فَإِنْ لَمْ يُجَاوِزْ دَمُهَا أَكْثَرَهُ اغْتَسَلَتْ أَيْضًا إِذَا انْقَطَعَ، فَإِنْ تَكَرَّرَ ثَلَاثًا فَهُوَ حَيْضٌ تَقْضِي مَا وَجَبَ فِيهِ، وَإِنْ أَيِسَتْ قَبْلَهُ، أَوْ لَمْ يَعُدْ فَلَا، وَإِنْ جَاوَزَهُ فَمُسْتَحَاضَةٌ تَجْلِسُ الْمُتَمَيِّزَ إِنْ كَانَ، وَصَلُحَ فِي الشَّهْرِ الثَّانِي، وَإِلَّا أَقَلَّ الْحَيْضِ حَتَّى تَتَكَرَّرَ اسْتِحَاضَتُهَا ثُمَّ غَالِبَهُ.

When a woman experiences her first period [menarche], she refrains [from all that must be avoided during menstruation] for the minimum duration ‹of menstruation (i.e., one day and night)›, then performs the purificatory bath and prays. If her bleeding does not exceed the maximum duration ‹by it stopping within fifteen days›, she bathes again when it stops. If this repeats three times, it is considered menstruation ‹and it is considered habitual›, and she makes up whatever was obligatory during it ‹including obligatory fasts, circumambulating for pilgrimage, and the like›. But if she reaches menopause or it never repeats, then it is not considered menstruation. If it exceeds the maximum amount ‹for menstruation› [i.e., fifteen days], she has irregular bleeding [*mustaḥāḍah*]. ‹Someone with irregular bleeding› that is differentiable in the second month refrains ‹from praying and fasting› if the blood fits menstruation – otherwise ‹if it is not distinctive, or none of it fits menstrual blood› she sits for the minimum duration of menstruation [one day and night] until her irregular bleeding repeats ‹three months [i.e., three times]› and she then sits for the most common duration ‹six or seven days›.

وَمُسْتَحَاضَةٌ مُعْتَادَةٌ تُقَدِّمُ عَادَتَهَا، وَيَلْزَمُهَا وَنَحْوَهَا غَسْلُ ٱلْمَحَلِّ وَعَصْبُهُ وَالْوُضُوءُ لِكُلِّ صَلَاةٍ إِنْ خَرَجَ شَيْءٌ، وَنِيَّةُ ٱلِاسْتِبَاحَةِ، وَحَرُمَ وَطْؤُهَا إِلَّا مَعَ خَوْفِ ٱلزِّنَا.

A woman with irregular bleeding who has a habitual cycle gives preference to her habit ‹even if the bleeding is differentiable›. She and people like her ‹e.g., someone with incontinence, perpetual flatulence, bleeding that does not clot, or nosebleeds› wash the place, apply a compress ‹i.e., plug or bind it to stop the flow›, make ablution for each prayer if anything exits, and intend being allowed [to perform acts requiring purification, *al-istibāḥah*]. It is unlawful to have intercourse with her except out of fear of fornication.

وَأَكْثَرُ مُدَّةِ ٱلنِّفَاسِ أَرْبَعُونَ يَوْمًا، وَالنَّقَاءُ زَمَنُهُ طُهْرٌ يُكْرَهُ ٱلْوَطْءُ فِيهِ، وَهُوَ كَحَيْضٍ فِي أَحْكَامِهِ غَيْرَ عِدَّةٍ وَبُلُوغٍ.

The maximum duration for lochia is forty days. Intermittent times of purity are considered purity; it is offensive to have intercourse during those times. Its rulings are like menstruation – except for the waiting period [*ʿiddah*] and reaching maturity.

2

PRAYER

كِتَابُ الصَّلَاةِ

Prayer Times

تَجِبُ ٱلْخَمْسُ عَلَى كُلِّ مُسْلِمٍ مُكَلَّفٍ إِلَّا حَائِضًا وَنُفَسَاءَ، وَلَا تَصِحُّ مِنْ مَجْنُونٍ وَلَا صَغِيرٍ غَيْرِ مُمَيِّزٍ وَعَلَى وَلِيِّهِ أَمْرُهُ بِهَا لِسَبْعٍ، وَضَرْبُهُ عَلَى تَرْكِهَا لِعَشْرٍ، وَيَحْرُمُ تَأْخِيرُهَا إِلَى وَقْتِ ٱلضَّرُورَةِ إِلَّا مِمَّنْ لَهُ ٱلْجَمْعُ بِنِيَّتِهِ، وَمُشْتَغِلٌ بِشَرْطٍ لَهَا يَحْصُلُ قَرِيبًا، وَجَاحِدُهَا كَافِرٌ.

The five prayers are obligatory for every responsible ‹i.e., physically mature and sane› Muslim except during menstruation and lochia.

Prayer is not valid from someone who is insane.

Prayer is not valid from someone who is a minor and lacks discernment. His guardian must command him to pray the five daily prayers on reaching seven lunar years of age, and discipline him for their omission on reaching ten years of age.

It is unlawful to delay prayers to their time of necessity [*waqt al-ḍarūrah*] except for someone who is eligible to combine prayers and intends to do so, or someone who is busy fulfilling one of its conditions and will achieve it shortly ‹e.g., ablution, the purificatory bath, someone busy patching a tear in their only garment›.

Whoever denies it ‹i.e, prayer› is a disbeliever. ‹So is someone who abandons prayer out of negligence or laziness, provided that the Imam or his deputy has called him to perform it and he refuses until the time for the next prayer draws to its end.›

The Call to Prayer

(فَصْلٌ) اَلْأَذَانُ وَالْإِقَامَةُ فَرْضَا كِفَايَةٍ عَلَى اَلرِّجَالِ اَلْأَحْرَارِ اَلْمُقِيمِينَ لِلْخَمْسِ اَلْمُؤَدَّاةِ وَالْجُمْعَةِ.

The call to prayer [*adhān*] and the call to its commencement [*iqāmah*] are community obligations [*farḍ*] on men who are free and resident for the current performance of the five [daily] ‹prayers› and for the Friday Prayer.

و لَا يَصِحُّ إِلَّا مُرَتَّبًا مُتَوَالِيًا مَنْوِيًّا مِنْ ذَكَرٍ مُمَيِّزٍ عَدْلٍ وَلَوْ ظَاهِرًا وَبَعْدَ اَلْوَقْتِ لِغَيْرِ فَجْرٍ وَسُنَّ كَوْنُهُ صَيِّتًا أَمِينًا عَالِمًا بِالْوَقْتِ

The call is not valid unless performed in order, consecutively and with intention; by a male who has discernment [*mumayyiz*], and is upright [*ʿadl*] ‹i.e., has not committed an enormity and does not persist in a lesser sin› – even if only apparently so; and after the time has entered (except for the Dawn Prayer ‹which is valid after half of the night has passed›).

It is recommended that the one performing it has a far-reaching voice, be trustworthy, and knows the time.

وَمَنْ جَمَعَ أَوْ قَضَى فَوَائِتَ أَذَّنَ لِلْأُولَى، وَأَقَامَ لِكُلِّ صَلَاةٍ.

Whoever combines or makes up prayers performs the call to prayer [*adhān*] for the first one and performs the call to commence prayer [*iqāmah*] for each one.

وَسُنَّ لِمُؤَذِّنٍ وَسَامِعِهِ مُتَابَعَةُ قَوْلِهِ سِرًّا إِلَّا فِي اَلْحَيْعَلَةِ، فَيَقُولُ: اَلْحَوْقَلَةَ وَفِي اَلتَّثْوِيبِ صَدَقْتَ وَبَرَرْتَ، وَالصَّلَاةُ عَلَى اَلنَّبِيِّ -عَلَيْهِ اَلسَّلَامُ- بَعْدَ فَرَاغِهِ، وَقَوْلُ مَا وَرَدَ وَالدُّعَاءُ.

It is recommended for the one making the call and whoever hears it to repeat what the caller says in an inaudible voice. But at "*ḥay ʿalā ṣ-ṣalāt*" ("Come to prayer") one says "*lā ḥawlah wa la quwwata illā bi-Llāh*" ("There is no power or strength except through Allah"), and at "*al-ṣalātu khayrun mina n-naum*" ("Prayer is better than sleep") one says "*ṣadaqta wa bararta*" ("You have spoken the truth, and piously").

‹It is recommended› [for them both] to supplicate for the Prophet ﷺ after it is finished, to say what was transmitted

› "*Allahumma rabb hadhihi al-daʾwati al-tāmmati wa al-ṣalāt al-qāimat, āti sayyidanā Muḥammadan al-wasīlah wa al-faḍīlah, wa-bʿathhu maqāman maḥmūdani lladhī waʿadatahu*"

("O Allah, Lord of this comprehensive invitation and enduring prayer, grant our liegelord Muḥammad a place near to You, an excellence and exalted degree, and bestow on him the praiseworthy station that You have promised him")›,

and to supplicate ‹here and after the call to commence prayer [*iqāmah*]›.

وَحَرُمَ خُرُوجٌ مِنْ مَسْجِدٍ بَعْدَهُ بِلَا عُذْرٍ أَوْ نِيَّةِ رُجُوعٍ.

It is unlawful to exit the mosque after it ‹i.e., the call to prayer, and before praying› without an excuse or intention to return.

Conditions for the Validity of Prayer

(فَصْلٌ) شُرُوطُ صِحَّةِ اَلصَّلَاةِ سِتَّةٌ:

طَهَارَةُ اَلْحَدَثِ وَتَقَدَّمْتْ، وَدُخُولُ اَلْوَقْتِ، فَوَقْتُ اَلظُّهْرِ مِنَ اَلزَّوَالِ حَتَّى يَتَسَاوَى مُنْتَصِبٌ وَفَيْؤُهُ سِوَى ظِلِّ اَلزَّوَالِ. وَيَلِيهِ اَلْمُخْتَارُ لِلْعَصْرِ حَتَّى يَصِيرَ ظِلُّ كُلِّ شَيْءٍ مِثْلَيْهِ، سِوَى ظِلِّ اَلزَّوَالِ، وَالضَّرُورَةُ إِلَى اَلْغُرُوبِ، وَيَلِيهِ اَلْمَغْرِبُ حَتَّى يَغِيبَ

اَلشَّفَقُ اَلْأَحْمَرُ، وَيَلِيهُ اَلْمُخْتَارُ لِلْعِشَاءِ إِلَى ثُلُثِ اَللَّيْلِ اَلْأَوَّلِ، وَالضَّرُورَةُ إِلَى طُلُوعِ فَجْرٍ ثَانٍ، وَيَلِيهِ اَلْفَجْرُ إِلَى اَلشُّرُوقِ.

The conditions for the validity of prayer are six.

‹The first is› being free of ritual impurity (mentioned earlier).

‹The second is› its time having entered. The time for Noon Prayer [*ẓuhr*] is from when the sun passes its zenith until the length of an object's shadow (minus its length at the zenith) equals its height. Following this is the preferred time for Afternoon Prayer [*ʿaṣr*], up until the shadow of every thing is twice its height (after subtracting its shadow at the zenith). Its time of necessity extends until sunset. Next is Sunset Prayer [*maghreb*], [which extends] until the red glow disappears. Following this is the preferred time for the Night Prayer [*ʿishā'*] [which extends] until the first third of the night. Its time of necessity extends until the second dawn ["true dawn," not "false dawn"]. Next is Morning Prayer [*fajr*], [which extends] up until sunrise.

وَتُدْرَكُ مَكْتُوبَةٌ بِإِحْرَامٍ فِي وَقْتِهَا، لَكِنْ يَحْرُمُ تَأْخِيرُهَا إِلَى وَقْتٍ لَا يَسَعُهَا، وَلَا يُصَلِّي حَتَّى يَتَيَقَّنَهُ أَوْ يَغْلِبَ عَلَى ظَنِّهِ دُخُولُهُ إِنْ عَجَزَ عَنِ اَلْيَقِينِ، وَيُعِيدُ إِنْ أَخْطَأَ.

An obligatory prayer is prayed on time if one says the initial "*Allāhu akbar*" ("Allah is most great!") within its time. However, it is unlawful to delay a prayer until the [remaining] time does not encompass it.

One does not pray until one is certain of the time or one thinks it is most likely that it has entered when certitude is not possible. One repeats the prayer if one was mistaken.

وَمَنْ صَارَ أَهْلًا لِوُجُوبِهَا قَبْلَ خُرُوجِ وَقْتِهَا بِتَكْبِيرَةٍ لَزِمَتْهُ، وَمَا يُجْمَعُ إِلَيْهَا قَبْلَهَا.

Whoever becomes qualified for its obligation [*ahlan li-wujūbihā*] before its time exits while enough time remains to say "*Allāhu akbar*" is required to perform it along with any prior prayer that can be joined with it ‹such as during travel. So if a minor matures or someone insane regains their sanity as the sun sets he would perform Noon and Afternoon Prayers, or if it happens when the horizon's red glow after sunset disappears he would pray Sunset and Night Prayers›.[1]

وَيَجِبُ فَوْرًا قَضَاءُ فَوَائِتَ مُرَتَّبًا مَا لَمْ يَتَضَرَّرْ أَوْ يَنْسَ أَوْ يَخْشَ فَوْتَ حَاضِرَةٍ أَوْ اِخْتِيَارِهَا.

It is obligatory to make up missed prayers immediately, in order, so long as doing so is not harmful, one has not forgotten ‹the order›, or one does not fear missing the current prayer or its preferred time.

اَلثَّالِثُ: سَتْرُ اَلْعَوْرَةِ، وَيَجِبُ حَتَّى خَارِجَهَا، وَفِي خَلْوَةٍ، وَفِي ظُلْمَةٍ بِمَا لَا يَصِفُ اَلْبَشَرَةَ.

The third ‹condition for prayer› is covering one's nakedness – it is obligatory even outside of prayer, when alone or in private places [*khalwah*], or in darkness – with something that does not characterize the skin ‹i.e., it being black or white; there is no harm if it conveys the shape›.

وَعَوْرَةُ رَجُلٍ وَحُرَّةٍ مُرَاهِقَةٍ وأَمَةٍ مَا بَيْنَ سُرَّةٍ وَرُكْبَةٍ، وَابْنِ سَبْعٍ إِلَى عَشْرٍ اَلْفَرْجَانِ، وَكُلُّ اَلْحُرَّةِ عَوْرَةٌ إِلَّا وَجْهَهَا فِي اَلصَّلَاةِ.

The nakedness of a man, a prepubescent female who is free, and a female slave is the area between the navel and the knees ‹though not the navel and the knees themselves›. ‹The nakedness of a› male between the ages of seven and ten [lunar years] is the private parts (front and rear). The nakedness of a free woman is her entire body – except for her face ‹and, according to groups of scholars, her hands› during prayer.

1. This is a general rule and it applies when the person is resident or traveling.

‹It is permissible to expose one's nakedness when necessary, such as for medical treatment, giving birth, and the like.›

وَمَنِ انْكَشَفَ بَعْضُ عَوْرَتِهِ وَفَحُشَ أَوْ صَلَّى فِي نَجِسٍ أَوْ غَصْبٍ ثَوْبًا أَوْ بُقْعَةً أَعَادَ، لَا مَنْ حُبِسَ فِي مَحَلٍّ نَجِسٍ (أَوْ غَصْبٍ) لَا يُمْكِنُهُ اَلْخُرُوجُ مِنْهُ.

One must repeat a prayer if one's nakedness was exposed for a lengthy period, or one prayed in filth or a stolen garment, or on stolen land. One does not repeat if one is confined to a filthy or stolen place and one is not able to leave.

اَلرَّابِعُ: اِجْتِنَابُ نَجَاسَةٍ غَيْرِ مَعْفُوٍّ عَنْهَا فِي بَدَنٍ وَثَوْبٍ وَبُقْعَةٍ مَعَ اَلْقُدْرَةِ.

The fourth ‹condition of prayer› is avoiding inexcusable filth on the body, clothes, and place of prayer – when able ‹to do so›.

وَمَنْ جَبَرَ عَظْمَهُ أَوْ خَاطَهُ بِنَجِسٍ وَتَضَرَّرَ بِقَلْعِهِ لَمْ يَجِبْ، وَيَتَيَمَّمُ إِنْ لَمْ يُغَطِّهِ اَللَّحْمُ.

Whenever filth is used to mend a bone or suture ‹a wound› and its removal would be harmful, it is not obligatory to do so. [In this case] one ‹obligatorily› makes dry ablution so long as flesh has not covered it ‹i.e., the break and its like; since it has not been washed with water›.

وَلَا تَصِحُّ بِلَا عُذْرٍ فِي مَقْبَرَةٍ وَخَلَاءٍ وَحَمَّامٍ وَأَعْطَانِ إِبِلٍ وَمَجْزَرَةٍ وَمَزْبَلَةٍ وَقَارِعَةِ طَرِيقٍ وَلَا فِي أَسْطِحَتِهَا

Prayer is not valid in graveyards, lavatories, bathhouses, camel pens, abattoirs, where trash is thrown ‹even if pure›, or the middle of the path – nor on their roofs.

اَلْخَامِسُ: اِسْتِقْبَالُ اَلْقِبْلَةِ، وَلَا تَصِحُّ بِدُونِهِ إِلَّا لِعَاجِزٍ وَمُتَنَفِّلٍ فِي سَفَرٍ مُبَاحٍ.

وَفَرْضُ قَرِيبٍ مِنْهَا إِصَابَةُ عَيْنِهَا، وَبَعِيدٍ جِهَتِهَا، وَيُعْمَلُ وُجُوبًا بِخَبَرِ ثِقَةٍ بِيَقِينٍ

وَبِمَحَارِيبِ ٱلْمُسْلِمِينَ، وَإِنِ ٱشْتَبَهَتْ فِي ٱلسَّفَرِ ٱجْتَهَدَ عَارِفٌ بِأَدِلَّتِهَا وَقَلَّدَ غَيْرُهُ إِنْ صَلَّى بِلَا أَحَدِهِمَا مَعَ (ٱلْقُدْرَةِ) قَضَى مُطْلَقًا.

The fifth ‹condition for prayer› is facing the direction of prayer. Prayer is not valid without it, except for someone unable to do so, or for someone performing voluntary prayers while on a lawful journey.

The obligation for someone close to the Kaʿbah is to face it exactly, and for someone distant is to face its direction.

It is obligatory to act according to the report of someone who is ‹a Muslim,› trustworthy ‹and responsible, visibly and inwardly upright› [whose report is] based on certainty, and according to the prayer niches [*maḥārīb*] of Muslims.

If, while traveling, the direction is not clear [*ishtabahat*], someone who knows its indicators exercises his personal judgment [*ijtahada*] and others ‹who do not knows its indicators› follow him.

Whoever prays without either of them ‹i.e., a trustworthy report or personal judgment› despite being able to do so must make it up, categorically [*muṭlaqan*] ‹whether they are in error or correct›.

ٱلسَّادِسُ: ٱلنِّيَّةُ، فَيَجِبُ تَعْيِينُ مُعَيَّنَةٍ وَسُنَّ مُقَارَنَتُهَا لِتَكْبِيرَةِ إِحْرَامٍ، وَلَا يَضُرُّ تَقْدِيمُهَا عَلَيْهَا بِيَسِيرٍ.

وَشُرِطَ نِيَّةُ إِمَامَةٍ وَٱئْتِمَامٍ، وَلِمُؤْتَمٍّ ٱنْفِرَادٌ لِعُذْرٍ، وَتَبْطُلُ صَلَاتُهُ بِبُطْلَانِ صَلَاةِ إِمَامِهِ، لَا عَكْسَ إِنْ نَوَى إِمَامٌ ٱلِانْفِرَادَ.

The sixth ‹condition for prayer› is intention. ‹Its conditions are being Muslim, sanity, and discernment. Its time is the beginning of an act of worship, or slightly before it.›

It is obligatory to identify personally-obligatory prayers. It is recommended for the intention to be made concurrent to the initial saying of "*Allāhu akbar,*" and there is no harm if it is made slightly beforehand.

Intention is a condition ‹for imams› to lead and ‹for followers› to follow. A follower can remove himself from following the imam when there is an excuse ‹permitting leaving the congregation, such as sickness, the prayer being lengthy›. A follower's prayer is invalidated if his imam's prayer is invalid – but not the opposite if an imam intends praying separately.

Description of the Prayer

يُسَنُّ خُرُوجُهُ إِلَيْهَا مُتَطَهِّرًا بِسَكِينَةٍ وَوَقَارٍ مَعَ قَوْلِ مَا وَرَدَ.

It is recommended that one goes out to it ‹i.e., to prayer› with purification, in a quiet and dignified manner; and with saying what was transmitted

‹"*Allāhumma innī as'aluka bi-ḥaqqi s-sā'ilīna ʿalayka, wa bi-ḥaqq mamshāya hādhā, fa innī lam akhruj asharan wa lā baṭaran, wa lā riā'an wa lā sumʿatan, wa kharajtu ittiqā'a sukhiṭka wa-btighā'a marḍātaka, fa as'aluka an tunqidhnī mina n-nār wa an taghfira lī dhunūbī, innahu lā yaghfiru dh-dhunūba illā anta*"

("O Allah, I ask You by the right that those who ask of You have over You, and I ask by the virtue of this walking of mine, for I am not exiting out of pride or vanity, or to show off or make a reputation. Rather, I exit out of fearing Your wrath and seeking Your pleasure. So I ask You to protect me from the Fire and to forgive me my sins, for no one can forgive sins save You")

"*Allāhumma-jʿalnī min awjahi man tawajjah ilayka, wa aqrabi man tawassala ilayka, wa afḍali man sa'alaka wa raghiba ilayka, Allāhumma-jʿalnī fī qalbī nūran, wa fī qabrī nūran, wa fī lisāni nūran, wa fī samʿī nūran, wa fī baṣarī nūran, wa ʿan yamīnī nūran, wa ʿan shimālī nūran, wa amāmī nūran, wa khalfī nūran, wa fauqī nūran, wa taḥtī nūran, wa fī ʿaṣabī nūran, wa fī laḥmī nūran, wa fī damī nūran, wa fī shaʿrī nūri, wa fī basharī nūran, wa fī nafsī nūran, wa ʿazim lī nūran, wa-jʿalnī nūran, Allāhumma ʿaṭinī nūran wa zidnī nūran*"

("O Allah, make me the best in those turning to You, and the closest who seek connection to You, and the best of those who ask of You and are desirous of You. O Allah, place light in my heart, light in my grave, light on my tongue, light in my hearing, light in my seeing, light on my right, light on my left, light before me, light behind me, light above me, light below me, light in my sinew, light in my flesh, light in my blood, light in my hair, light in my skin, light in my self. Make the light greater for me. Make me light. O Allah, grant me a light and increase me in light!")›.

وَقِيَامُ إِمَامٍ، فَغَيْرُ مُقِيمٍ إِلَيْهَا عِنْدَ قَوْلِ مُقِيمٍ: «قَدْ قَامَتْ ٱلصَّلَاةُ»، فَيَقُولُ: «ٱللهُ أَكْبَرُ» وَهُوَ قَائِمٌ فِي فَرْضٍ رَافِعًا يَدَيْهِ إِلَى حَذْوِ مَنْكِبَيْهِ ثُمَّ يَقْبِضُ بِيُمْنَاهُ كُوعَ يُسْرَاهُ وَيَجْعَلُهُمَا تَحْتَ سُرَّتِهِ، وَيَنْظُرُ مَسْجِدَهُ فِي كُلِّ صَلَاتِهِ ثُمَّ يَقُولُ: «سُبْحَانَكَ ٱللَّهُمَّ وَبِحَمْدِكَ، وَتَبَارَكَ اسْمُكَ وَتَعَالَى جَدُّكَ، وَلَا إِلَهَ غَيْرُكَ». ثُمَّ يَسْتَعِيذُ ثُمَّ يُبَسْمِلُ (سِرًّا).

‹It is recommended› for the imam and then others who are not standing to stand when the person making the call to commence prayer says, "*Qad qāmati ṣ-ṣalāh.*"

One then says "*Allāhu akbar,*" while standing (for obligatory [*farḍ*] prayers) and raising one's hands parallel to his shoulders. One then grasps above one's left wrist [*kūʿ*] with the right hand, places them below the navel, and throughout the prayer looks at the place of prostration. One then says

"*Subḥānaka Llāhumma wa bi-ḥamdika wa tabārak ismuka wa taʿālā jadduka wa lā ilāha ghayruka*"

("Glory and praise be to You, O Allah, blessed be Your Name and exalted be Your majesty, none has the right to be worshipped but you")

then seeks protection ‹saying "*aʿūdhu bi-Llāhi mina sh-shayṭāni r-rajīm*" ("I take refuge from the accursed Devil")›, and says "*Bismi Llāhi r-raḥmāni r-raḥīm*" ("In the name of Allah, most Merciful, and Compassionate") – inaudibly ‹in all of them›.

ثُمَّ يَقْرَأُ ٱلْفَاتِحَةَ مُرَتَّبَةً مُتَوَالِيَةً، وَفِيهَا إِحْدَى عَشْرَةَ تشديدةً، وَإِذَا فَرَغَ قَالَ: «آمِينَ» يَجْهَرُ بِهَا إِمَامٌ وَمَأْمُومٌ مَعًا فِي جَهْرِيَّةٍ وَغَيْرُهُمَا فِيمَا يُجْهَرُ فِيهِ.

One then recites Al-Fātiḥah [Q1], in order and consecutively. It contains eleven *shaddah*s. When finished, one says "*Āmīn*": the imam and followers say it together audibly in audible prayers. Others ‹i.e., those praying individually› say it audibly in whatever is prayed audibly.

وَيُسَنُّ جَهْرُ إِمَامٍ بِقِرَاءَةِ صُبْحٍ وَجُمُعَةٍ وَعِيدٍ وَكُسُوفٍ وَاسْتِسْقَاءٍ، وَأُولَيَيْ مَغْرِبٍ وَعِشَاءٍ، وَيُكْرَهُ لِمَأْمُومٍ، وَيُخَيَّرُ مُنْفَرِدٌ وَنَحْوُهُ

It is recommended for the imam to recite audibly in the Dawn, Friday, Eid, Lunar Eclipse [*kusūf*] and Draught Prayers; and in the first two [prayer-cycles] of Sunset and Night Prayers. It is offensive for a follower to recite audibly. Individuals and their like ‹e.g. someone making up prayers› can choose ‹between being audible and inaudible›.

ثُمَّ يَقْرَأُ بَعْدَهَا سُورَةً فِي ٱلصُّبْحِ مِنْ طِوَالِ ٱلْمُفَصَّلِ وَٱلْمَغْرِبِ مِنْ قِصَارِهِ، وَٱلْبَاقِي مِنْ أَوْسَاطِهِ.

After Al-Fātiḥah [Q1], one then recites a chapter [*sūrah*]. One reads from the longer "*mufaṣṣal*" *sūrah*s ‹from Qāf [Q50] through

ʿAmma [Q78]› at Dawn Prayer, the shorter ones ‹Ḍuḥā [93] to the end [Q114]› during Sunset Prayer, and the mid-length ones ‹ʿAmma [Q78] thorough Ḍuḥā [93]› during the remaining prayers.

ثُمَّ يَرْكَعُ مُكَبِّرًا رَافِعًا يَدَيْهِ، ثُمَّ يَضَعُهُمَا عَلَى رُكْبَتَيْهِ مُفَرَّجَتَيِ ٱلْأَصَابِعِ وَيُسَوِّي ظَهْرَهُ، وَيَقُولُ: «سُبْحَانَ رَبِّيَ ٱلْعَظِيمِ» ثَلَاثًا، وَهُوَ أَدْنَى ٱلْكَمَالِ.

One then bows while saying "*Allāhu akbar*" and raising one's hands. One then places one's hands on the knees, fingers spread apart, and the back straight. One says, "*Subḥāna rabbī al-ʿaẓīm*" ("Glory be to my Lord Almighty") three times (which is the minimum complete amount).

ثُمَّ يَرْفَعُ رَأْسَهُ وَيَدَيْهِ مَعَهُ قَائِلًا: «سَمِعَ ٱللهُ لِمَنْ حَمِدَهُ» وَبَعْدَ ٱنْتِصَابِهِ: «رَبَّنَا وَلَكَ ٱلْحَمْدُ مِلْءَ ٱلسَّمَاءِ وَمِلْءَ ٱلْأَرْضِ وَمِلْءَ مَا شِئْتَ مِنْ شَيْءٍ بَعْدُ» وَمَأْمُومٌ: «رَبَّنَا وَلَكَ ٱلْحَمْدُ» فَقَطْ.

One then raises one's head and hands together, saying "*Samiʿa Llāhu li-man ḥamidah*" ("Allah hears whoever praises him"), and then "*rabbanā laka l-ḥamd*" ("Our Lord, all praise is yours"). Once one is erect, one says

> "*rabbanā laka l-ḥamd milʾa s-samāʾ wa milʾa l-arḍ wa milʾa mā shiʾta min shayʾin baʿd*"
>
> ("Our Lord, all praise is yours, [a praise] that would fill the heavens and the earth and fill that which pleases Thee besides them!").

Followers say only "*rabbanā laka l-ḥamd.*"

ثُمَّ يُكَبِّرُ وَيَسْجُدُ عَلَى ٱلْأَعْضَاءِ ٱلسَّبْعَةِ، فَيَضَعُ رُكْبَتَيْهِ ثُمَّ يَدَيْهِ ثُمَّ جَبْهَتَهُ وَأَنْفَهُ.

One then says "*Allāhu akbar*" and prostrates on the seven limbs: one places ‹first› one's knees, and then one's hands, then one's forehead, and then one's nose.

وَسُنَّ كَوْنُهُ عَلَى أَطْرَافِ أَصَابِعِهِ وَمُجَافَاةُ عَضُدَيْهِ عَنْ جَنْبَيْهِ، وَبَطْنُهُ عَنْ فَخِذَيْهِ، وَتَفْرِقَةُ رُكْبَتَيْهِ وَيَقُولُ: «سُبْحَانَ رَبِّيَ ٱلْأَعْلَى» ثَلَاثًا، وَهِيَ أَدْنَى (ٱلْكَمَالِ).

It is recommended that prostration be done upon the tips of one's toes, spreading the forearms out from one's flanks and one's stomach away from one's thighs, and one's knees separated. One says, "*subḥān rabbī al-aʿlā*" ("Glory be to my Lord Most High") three times (which is the minimum complete amount).

ثُمَّ يَرْفَعُ مُكَبِّرًا وَيَجْلِسُ مُفْتَرِشًا وَيَقُولُ: «رَبِّ اغْفِرْ لِي» ثَلَاثًا، وَهُوَ أَكْمَلُهُ،

One then rises while saying "*Allāhu akbar,*" sits *muftarishan* ‹sitting with the left foot below one's buttocks while the right foot is raised up with the toes on the ground pointing towards the direction of prayer›, and says, "*rabbi-ghfir lī*" ("My Lord, forgive me") three times (which is the complete amount).

وَيَسْجُدُ ٱلثَّانِيَةَ كَذَلِكَ،

One then prostrates the second time the same way.

ثُمَّ يَنْهَضُ مُعْتَمِدًا عَلَى رُكْبَتَيْهِ بِيَدَيْهِ، فَإِنْ شَقَّ فَبِالْأَرْضِ، فَيَأْتِي بِمِثْلِهِ غَيْرَ ٱلنِّيَّةِ والتحريمةِ وَالِاسْتِفْتَاحِ وَالتَّعَوُّذِ، إِنْ كَانَ تَعَوَّذَ ثُمَّ يَجْلِسُ مُفْتَرِشًا.

One then rises, saying "*Allāhu akbar,*" supporting himself by putting his hands on the knees. (If this is difficult, one supports oneself by putting the hands on the ground.)

One does ‹a prayer-cycle with› the same ‹as the first›, except for the intention, initial "*Allāhu akbar,*" opening supplication, and seeking protection from Satan (if already done).

Then ‹after performing the prayer-cycle› once sits *muftarishan.*

وَسُنَّ وَضْعُ يَدَيْهِ عَلَى فَخِذَيْهِ وَقَبْضُ ٱلْخِنْصَرِ وَالْبِنْصَرِ مِنْ يُمْنَاهُ، وَتَحْلِيقُ إِبْهَامِهِمَا مَعَ ٱلْوُسْطَى، وَإِشَارَتُهُ بِسَبَّابَتِهَا فِي تَشَهُّدٍ وَدُعَاءٍ عِنْدَ ذِكْرِ ٱللهِ مُطْلَقًا وَبَسْطُ ٱلْيُسْرَى، ثُمَّ يَتَشَهَّدُ فَيَقُولُ: «ٱلتَّحِيَّاتُ لِلهِ، وَالصَّلَوَاتُ ٱلطَّيِّبَاتُ، ٱلسَّلَامُ عَلَيْكَ أَيُّهَا ٱلنَّبِيُّ وَرَحْمَةُ ٱللهِ وَبَرَكَاتُهُ، ٱلسَّلَامُ عَلَيْنَا وَعَلَى عِبَادِ ٱللهِ ٱلصَّالِحِينَ، أَشْهَدُ أَنْ لَا إِلَهَ إِلَّا ٱللهُ، وَأَشْهَدُ أَنَّ مُحَمَّدًا عَبْدُهُ وَرَسُولُهُ».

It is recommended to place one's hand on one's thighs, closing the two smallest fingers and forming a circle with the thumb and middle finger, and pointing with the index finger during the *tashahhud* and supplication whenever mentioning "*Allāh.*" ‹It is also recommended› to extend the fingers of the left hand. One then says the *tashahhud,* saying:

> "*Al-Taḥiyyātu li-Llāhi wa ṣ-ṣalawātu wa t-ṭayyibāt, al-salāmu ʿalayka ayyuha n-nabī wa raḥmatu Llāhi wa barakātuhu, al-salāmu ʿalaynā wa ʿalā ʿibādi Llāhi ṣ-ṣāliḥin, ashhadu an lā ilāha illa Llāhu, wa-ashhadu anna Muḥammadan ʿabduhu wa rasūluhu*"
>
> ("Greetings to Allah, and prayers and goodness. Peace be upon you, O Prophet, and the mercy of Allah and His blessings. Peace be upon us and upon the righteous servants of Allah. I testify that there is no deity except Allah, and I testify that Muḥammad is His servant and Messenger").

ثُمَّ يَنْهَضُ فِي مَغْرِبٍ وَرُبَاعِيَّةٍ مُكَبِّرًا وَيُصَلِّي ٱلْبَاقِي كَذَلِكَ سِرًّا مُقْتَصِرًا عَلَى ٱلْفَاتِحَةِ، ثُمَّ يَجْلِسُ مُتَوَرِّكًا فَيَأْتِي بِالتَّشَهُّدِ ٱلْأَوَّلِ، ثُمَّ يَقُولُ: «ٱللَّهُمَّ صَلِّ عَلَى مُحَمَّدٍ وَعَلَى

آلِ مُحَمَّدٍ كَمَا صَلَّيْتَ عَلَى إِبْرَاهِيمَ وَعَلَى آلِ إِبْرَاهِيمَ إِنَّكَ حَمِيدٌ مَجِيدٌ، وَبَارِكْ عَلَى مُحَمَّدٍ وَعَلَى آلِ مُحَمَّدٍ كَمَا بَارَكْتَ عَلَى إِبْرَاهِيمَ وَعَلَى آلِ إِبْرَاهِيمَ إِنَّكَ حَمِيدٌ مَجِيدٌ»، وَسُنَّ أَنْ يَتَعَوَّذَ فَيَقُولَ: «أَعُوذُ بِاللهِ مِنْ عَذَابِ جَهَنَّمَ، وَمِنْ عَذَابِ اَلْقَبْرِ، وَمِنْ فِتْنَةِ اَلْمَحْيَا وَالْمَمَاتِ وَمِنْ فِتْنَةِ اَلْمَسِيحِ اَلدَّجَّالِ، اَللَّهُمَّ أَعُوذُ بِكَ مِنْ اَلْمَأْثَمِ وَالْمَغْرَمِ» وَتَبْطُلُ بِدُعَاءٍ بِأَمْرِ اَلدُّنْيَا ثُمَّ يَقُولُ عَنْ يَمِينِهِ ثُمَّ عِنْ يَسَارِهِ: «اَلسَّلَامُ عَلَيْكُمْ وَرَحْمَةُ اَللهِ»، مُرَتَّبًا مُعَرَّفًا وُجُوبًا.

One then rises in the Sunset Prayer and in prayers with four prayer-cycles, saying "*Allāhu akbar,*" and prays the rest of the prayer the same way – though inaudibly and reciting just Al-Fātiḥah.

Then one sits *mutawarrikan* ‹similar to *iftirāsh* except that the left foot goes out under the right shin, and the bottom of the left thigh and buttocks are in contact with the ground›, repeats the first *tashahhud*, and then says:

> "*Allāhumma ṣalli ʿalā Muḥammadin wa ʿalā āli Muḥammadin kamā ṣallayta ʿalā ibrāhīma wa ʿalā āli Ibrāhīma innaka ḥamīdun majīd, wa bārik ʿalā Muḥammadin wa ʿalā āli Muḥammadin kamā bārakta ʿalāIbrāhīmawaʿalāāliIbrāhīmainnakaḤamīdunmajīd*"
>
> ("O Allah, bless Muḥammad and the folk of Muḥammad as you blessed Ibrāhīm and the family of Ibrahim, for You are truly the Most Praiseworthy and Noble. O Allah, show grace to Muḥammad and the folk of Muḥammad as You did to Ibrāhīm and the family of Ibrahim in the worlds, for You are truly the Most Praiseworthy and Noble").

It is recommended to seek protection by saying:

> "*aʿūdhu bi-Llāhi min ʿadhābi jahannama wa min ʿadhābi l-qabri wa min fitnati l-maḥyā wa l-mamāt wa min fitnati l-masīḥi d-dajjāl, Allāhumma innī aʿūdhu bika mina l-maʾthami wa l-maghram*"

("O Allah, I seek refuge with You from the torment of the Hellfire, from the torment of the grave, from the trial of life and death, and from the evil of the trial of the Anti-Christ. O Allah, I seek refuge with Thee from sin and debt").

It ‹the prayer› is invalidated by supplication for a [purely] worldly affair.

One then says to the right and then the left: "*as-sālamu ʿalaykum wa raḥmatu Llāh*" ("Peace be upon you, and the Mercy of Allah"). It is obligatory for it to be in order and [the "*salāmu*"] to be with "*al-*".

وَامْرَأَةٌ كَرَجُلٍ، لَكِنْ تَجْمَعُ نَفْسَهَا، وَتَجْلِسُ مُتَرَبِّعَةً، أَوْ مُسْدِلَةً رِجْلَيْهَا عَنْ يَمِينِهَا وَهُوَ أَفْضَلُ.

A woman is like a man ‹with regards to the previous description of prayer› except that she bunches herself together, sits with her legs underneath her or slid underneath her slightly to the right (which is best).

وَكُرِهَ فِيهَا الْتِفَاتٌ وَنَحْوُهُ بِلَا حَاجَةٍ وَإِقْعَاءٌ، وَافْتِرَاشُ ذِرَاعَيْهِ سَاجِدًا، وَعَبَثٌ وَتَخَصُّرٌ وَفَرْقَعَةُ أَصَابِعَ وَتَشْبِيكُهَا، وَكَوْنُهُ حَاقِنًا وَنَحْوَهُ، وَتَائِقًا لِطَعَامٍ وَنَحْوِهِ.

During ‹the prayer› it is offensive to turn ‹slightly› or the like without need ‹such as out of fear or sickness›; to sit on the back of one's ankles with the buttocks and one's palms on the ground; to place all of one's forearms on the ground during prostration; to fidget; to place one's hands on both hips; to pop one's knuckles; and to interlace one's fingers.

‹It is offensive to pray while› one needs to urinate or the like ‹e.g., holding back feces or flatulence›, or when desirous of food or the like ‹e.g., drink or sex›.

وَإِذَا نَابَهُ شَيْءٌ سَبَّحَ رَجُلٌ، وَصَفَّقَتْ اِمْرَأَةٌ بِبَطْنِ كَفِّهَا عَلَى ظَهْرِ اَلْأُخْرَى، وَيُزِيلُ بُصَاقًا وَنَحْوَهُ بِثَوْبِهِ، وَيُبَاحُ فِي غَيْرِ مَسْجِدٍ عَنْ يَسَارِهِ، وَيُكْرَهُ أَمَامَهُ وَيَمِينَهُ.

If something occurs during prayer ‹like someone seeking permission or the imam forgetting an obligation›, men say "*subḥān Allāh*" and women clap the palm of one hand on the back of the other.

One ‹who is praying› removes phlegm and the like ‹e.g., nasal discharge› with one's garment. Outside the mosque, it is permissible to expel it on to one's left; it is offensive to do so in front of oneself or on one's right.

Its Essential & Obligatory Elements

(فَصْلٌ) وَجُمْلَةُ أَرْكَانِهَا أَرْبَعَةَ عَشَرَ:

اَلْقِيَامُ، والتحريمةُ وَالْفَاتِحَةُ، وَالرُّكُوعُ، وَالِاعْتِدَالُ عَنْهُ، وَالسُّجُودُ، وَالِاعْتِدَالُ عَنْهُ، وَالْجُلُوسُ بَيْنَ اَلسَّجْدَتَيْنِ، وَالطُّمَأْنِينَةُ وَالتَّشَهُّدُ اَلْأَخِيرُ، وَجِلْسَتُهُ، وَالصَّلَاةُ عَلَى اَلنَّبِيِّ عَلَيْهِ اَلسَّلَامُ، وَالتَّسْلِيمَتَانِ، وَالتَّرْتِيبُ.

The elements of the prayer that are essential [*rukn*, pl. *arkān*] are fourteen:

‹1› standing ‹in obligatory prayers but not in recommended prayers›;
‹2› saying the inaugural "*Allāhu akbar*";
‹3› ‹reciting› Al-Fātiḥah;
‹4–5› bowing and rising from it;
‹6–7› prostrating and rising from it;
‹8–9› sitting between the two prostrations and reposing;
‹10–11› the final *tashahhud* and sitting for it;
‹12› supplicating for the Prophet ﷺ;
‹13› the two sayings of "*al-salām ʿalaykum*"; and,
‹14› the order ‹between the essential elements as they were mentioned here and in the [forthcoming] description of prayer›.

وَوَاجِبَاتُهَا ثَمَانِيَةٌ: اَلتَّكْبِيرُ غَيْرَ التحريمةِ، وَالتَّسْمِيعُ، وَالتَّحْمِيدُ، وَتَسْبِيحُ رُكُوعٍ وَسُجُودٍ، وَقَوْلُ: «رَبِّ اِغْفِرْ لِي»، مَرَّةً مَرَّةً وَالتَّشَهُّدُ اَلْأَوَّلُ، وَجِلْسَتُهُ. وَمَا عَدَا ذَلِكَ وَالشُّرُوطُ سُنَّةٌ. فَالرُّكْنُ وَالشَّرْطُ لَا يَسْقُطَانِ سَهْوًا وَجَهْلاً، وَيَسْقُطُ اَلْوَاجِبُ بِهِمَا.

The elements of the prayer that are obligatory [*wājib*, pl. *wājibāt*] are eight:
‹1› the sayings of "*Allāhu akbar*" other than the initial one;
‹2–3› saying "*samiʿa Allāhu li man ḥamidah*" and "*rabbanā laka l-ḥamd,*"
‹4–6› saying "*subḥānu Llāh*" during bowing and prostration, and saying "*rabbi ghfir lī*" – one time each; and,
‹7–8› the first *tashahhud* and sitting for it.

Everything other than these and the conditions for prayer are recommended acts.

The essential elements and conditions of prayer are never dropped out of forgetfulness or ignorance, though obligatory elements cease being obligatory for both [reasons].

The Prostration of Forgetfulness

(فَصْلٌ) وَيُشْرَعُ سُجُودُ اَلسَّهْوِ لِزِيَادَةٍ وَنَقْصٍ وَشَكٍّ، لَا فِي عَمْدٍ، وَهُوَ وَاجِبٌ لِمَا تَبْطُلُ بِتَعَمُّدِهِ وَسُنَّةٌ لِإِتْيَانٍ بِقَوْلٍ مَشْرُوعٍ فِي غَيْرِ مَحَلِّهِ سَهْوًا، وَلَا تَبْطُلُ بِتَعَمُّدِهِ، وَمُبَاحٌ لِتَرْكِ سُنَّةٍ.

The prostration of forgetfulness is legislated ‹–it being obligatory or recommended–› for an addition, deletion, and doubt – but not for a deliberate action.

The prostration is obligatory for anything that, when performed deliberately, would invalidate the prayer ‹e.g., saying "*al-salāmu ʿalaykum*" prematurely, or adding a bowing, prostration or the like›.

The prostration is recommended for forgetfully making an utterance out of its proper place. Doing so deliberately does not invalidate the prayer.

The prostration is permissible [*mubāḥ*] for omitting a recommendation.

وَمَحَلُّهُ قَبْلَ ٱلسَّلَامِ نَدْبًا إِلَّا إِذَا سَلَّمَ عَنْ نَقْصِ رَكْعَةٍ فَأَكْثَرَ فَبَعْدَهُ نَدْبًا.

It is recommended for it ‹the prostration for an addition or doubt› to occur before saying "*al-salāmu ʿalaykum*" unless one said "*al-salāmu ʿalaykum*" prematurely by one or more prayer-cycles – in which case it is recommended to come after.

وَإِنْ سَلَّمَ قَبْلَ إِتْمَامِهَا عَمْدًا بَطَلَتْ، وَسَهْوًا فَإِنْ ذَكَرَ قَرِيبًا أَتَمَّهَا وَسَجَدَ.

If one deliberately says "*al-salāmu ʿalaykum*" before finishing the prayer, the prayer is invalidated. If one forgetfully said it and soon remembers it, one completes the prayer and prostrates ‹for forgetfulness›.

وَإِنْ أَحْدَثَ أَوْ قَهْقَهَ بَطَلَتْ كَفِعْلِهِمَا فِي صُلْبِهَا، وَإِنْ نَفَخَ أَوْ اِنْتَحَبَ لَا مِنْ خَشْيَةِ اللهِ، أَوْ تَنَحْنَحَ بِلَا حَاجَةٍ فَبَانَ حَرْفَانِ بَطَلَتْ، وَمَنْ تَرَكَ رُكْنًا غَيْرَ التحريمةِ فَذَكَرَهُ بَعْدَ شُرُوعِهِ فِي قِرَاءَةِ رَكْعَةٍ أُخْرَى بَطَلَتْ ٱلْمَتْرُوكُ مِنْهَا، وَصَارَتْ ٱلَّتِي شَرَعَ فِي قِرَاءَتِهَا مَكَانَهَا، وَقَبْلَهُ يَعُودُ فَيَأْتِي بِهِ وَبِمَا بَعْدَهُ، وَبَعْدَ سَلَامٍ فَكَتَرْكِ رَكْعَةٍ.

If one ‹who forgetfully said it before finishing the prayer and› lost ablution or laughed ‹after prematurely ending the prayer›, the prayer is invalidated – just like their occurrence within the prayer. ‹Speech in all circumstances invalidates prayer.›

The prayer is invalidated if one blows, wails (but not out of fear of Allah), or clears the throat and produces two phonemes.

Whoever missed an essential element [*rukn*] other than the initial "*Allāhu akbar*" and then remembers it after beginning the recitation in another prayer-cycle: the prayer-cycle with the skipped element is invalidated, and the prayer-cycle whose recitation he has begun takes its place. ‹If one remembers the omitted element› before ‹beginning the recitation in another prayer-cycle›, one returns ‹to it – obligatorily› and performs it and whatever follows it. ‹If one does not remember it except› after the closing "*al-salāmu ʿalaykum,*" it is akin to omitting a ‹complete› prayer-cycle. ‹So one performs a prayer-cycle and makes the prostration of forgetfulness provided the separation is not lengthy and one did not lose their purification or speak.›

وَإِنْ نَهَضَ عَنْ تَشَهُّدٍ أَوَّلَ نَاسِيًا لَزِمَ رُجُوعُهُ وَكُرِهَ إِنْ اِسْتَتَمَّ قَائِمًا، وَحَرُمَ وَبَطَلَتْ إِنْ شَرَعَ فِي اَلْقِرَاءَةِ لَا إِنْ نَسِيَ أَوْ جَهِلَ، وَيَتْبَعُ مَأْمُومٌ وَيَجِبُ اَلسُّجُودُ لِذَلِكَ مُطْلَقًا.

If one rises forgetfully without making the first *tashahhud* ‹if one remembers before rising completely›, one is required to return to it. It is offensive ‹to return to it› if one has completely stood up. It is unlawful and invalidates ‹the prayer› [to return] if one has ‹knowingly and deliberately› stood and begun reciting – but not if one is forgetful or ignorant ‹of the unlawfulness of returning›.

Followers follow their imam, and making the prostration of forgetfulness for it is always obligatory.

وَيَبْنِي عَلَى اَلْيَقِينِ –وَهُوَ اَلْأَقَلُّ– مَنْ شَكَّ فِي رُكْنٍ أَوْ عَدَدٍ.

Someone who doubts performing an essential element or the number ‹of prayer-cycles› builds upon their certainty (which is the least amount).

Voluntary Prayers

(فَصْلٌ) آكَدُ صَلَاةِ تَطَوُّعٍ: كُسُوفٌ فَاسْتِسْقَاءٌ فتراويحُ فَوِتْرٌ.

وَوَقْتُهُ مِنْ صَلَاةِ اَلْعِشَاءِ إِلَى اَلْفَجْرِ، وَأَقَلُّهُ رَكْعَةٌ، وَأَكْثَرُهُ إِحْدَى عَشْرَةَ: مَثْنَى مَثْنَى، وَيُوتِرُ بِوَاحِدَةٍ، وَأَدْنَى اَلْكَمَالِ ثَلَاثٌ بِسَلَامَيْنِ، وَيَقْنُتُ بَعْدَ اَلرُّكُوعِ نَدْبًا، فَيَقُولُ: «اَللَّهُمَّ اِهْدِنِي فِيمَنْ هَدَيْتَ وَعَافِنِي فِيمَنْ عَافَيْتَ، وَتَوَلَّنِي فِيمَنْ تَوَلَّيْتَ، وَبَارِكْ لِي فِيمَا أَعْطَيْتَ، وَقِنِي شَرَّ مَا قَضَيْتَ، إِنَّكَ تَقْضِي وَلَا يُقْضَى عَلَيْكَ، إِنَّهُ لَا يَذِلُّ مَنْ

وَالَيْتَ، وَلَا يَعِزُّ مَنْ عَادَيْتَ، تَبَارَكْتَ رَبَّنَا وَتَعَالَيْتَ، اَللَّهُمَّ إِنَّا نَعُوذُ بِرِضَاكَ مِنْ سُخْطِكَ، وَبِعَفْوِكَ مِنْ عُقُوبَتِكَ، وَبِكَ مِنْكَ لَا نُحْصِي ثَنَاءً عَلَيْكَ أَنْتَ كَمَا أَثْنَيْتَ عَلَى نَفْسِكَ» ثُمَّ يُصَلِّي عَلَى النَّبِيِّ ﷺ وَيُؤَمِّنُ مَأْمُومٌ، وَيَجْمَعُ إِمَامٌ اَلضَّمِيرَ وَيَمْسَحُ اَلدَّاعِي وَجْهَهُ بِيَدَيْهِ مُطْلَقًا.

The most emphatically recommended voluntary prayers are the Eclipse Prayer, Drought Prayer, Tarawih Prayer, and then Witr Prayer.

The time for Witr Prayer is from praying Night Prayer up until dawn. Its minimum amount is one prayer-cycle. Its maximum is eleven, prayed two prayer-cycles at a time with a single prayer-cycle at the end. The minimum optimal amount is three prayer-cycles with two [separate] sayings of "*al-salāmu ʿalaykum.*"

It is recommended [*nadban*] to make the *Qunūt* Supplication after the ‹last› bowing. One says,

> "*Allāhumma ihdinī fīman hadayt, wa ʿāfinī fīman ʿāfayt, wa tawallanī fīman tawallayt, wa bārik lī fīmā aʿṭayt, wa qinī sharra mā qaḍayt, innaka taqḍī wa lā yuqḍā ʿalayk, innahu lā yadhillu man wālayta, wa lā yaʿizzu man ʿādayta, tabārakta rabbanā wa taʿālayta. Allāhumma innā naʿūdhu bi-riḍāka min sakhaṭika wa bi-ʿafwika min ʿuqūbatika wa bika minka, lā nuḥṣī thanāʾan ʿalayka anta kamā athnayta ʿalā nafsika*"
>
> ("O Allah, guide me among those You have guided, grant me security among those You have granted security, take me into Your charge among those You have taken into Your charge, bless me in what You have given, guard me from the evil of what You have decreed, for You do decree, and nothing is decreed for You. None is abased whom you befriend. And none is exalted whom you are at enmity with. Blessed and Exalted are You, our Lord. O Allah, I seek refuge in Your pleasure from Your wrath, and I seek refuge in Your forgiveness from Your punishment, and I seek refuge in You from You. We cannot enumerate Your praise, You are as You have praised Yourself").

One then supplicates for the Prophet ﷺ.
Followers say "*Amīn.*" The imam pluralizes the pronoun.
A supplicant wipes his face with his hands, categorically [*muṭlaqan*] ‹i.e., the imam and others, and after every supplication in prayer and outside of prayer›.

وَالتَّرَاوِيحُ عِشْرُونَ رَكْعَةً بِرَمَضَانَ تُسَنُّ، وَالْوِتْرُ مَعَهَا جَمَاعَةً، وَوَقْتُهَا بَيْنَ سُنَّةِ عِشَاءٍ وَوِتْرٍ.

The Tarawih Prayer is twenty prayer-cycles [in length] during Ramadan. It, along with Witr, are recommended to be prayed in congregation. Its time is between the performances of the Night Prayer's recommended prayer and Witr.

ثُمَّ اَلرَّاتِبَةُ رَكْعَتَانِ قَبْلَ اَلظُّهْرِ، وَرَكْعَتَانِ بَعْدَهَا، وَرَكْعَتَانِ بَعْدَ اَلْمَغْرِبِ، وَرَكْعَتَانِ بَعْدَ اَلْعِشَاءِ، وَرَكْعَتَانِ قَبْلَ اَلْفَجْرِ، وَهُمَا آكَدُهَا وَتُسَنُّ صَلَاةُ اَللَّيْلِ بِتَأَكُّدٍ، وَهِيَ أَفْضَلُ مِنْ صَلَاةِ اَلنَّهَارِ.

The voluntary prayers associated with the obligatory prayers [*rawātib*] are two prayer-cycles before and after Noon Prayer; two after Sunset Prayer; two after Night Prayer; and two before Dawn Prayer. (These ‹the two for Dawn Prayer› are the most emphatically recommended).
Praying ‹categorically voluntary prayers› at night is emphatically recommended. It ‹praying at night› is superior to praying during the day. ‹And after sleeping is more superior.›

وَسُجُودُ تِلَاوَةٍ لِقَارِئٍ وَمُسْتَمِعٍ وَيُكَبِّرُ إِذَا سَجَدَ وَإِذَا رَكَعَ وَيَجْلِسُ وَيُسَلِّمُ، وَكُرِهَ لِإِمَامٍ قِرَاءَتُهَا فِي سِرِّيَّةٍ وَسُجُودُهُ لَهَا وَعَلَى مَأْمُومٍ مُتَابَعَتُهُ فِي غَيْرِهَا.

The Prostration for Recitation is for the reciter and whoever listens. One says "*Allāhu akbar*" when prostrating and when rising. One sits and says, "*as-salāmu ʿalaykum.*" It is offensive for an imam to recite it ‹a verse of prostration› during an inaudible prayer and his prostrating for doing so [is also offensive and a follower is not required to follow him in it]. A follower must follow the imam['s prostration for recitation] in audible prayers.

وَسُجُودُ شُكْرٍ عِنْدَ تَجَدُّدِ نِعَمٍ، وَانْدِفَاعِ نِقَمٍ، وَتَبْطُلُ بِهِ صَلَاةُ غَيْرِ جَاهِلٍ وَنَاسٍ، وَهُوَ كَسُجُودِ تِلَاوَةٍ.

The Prostration for Thanks is ‹recommended› when a blessing occurs or an affliction is removed. Prayer is invalidated by it – except for someone who is ignorant or forgetful. It is like the Prostration of Recitation ‹in its description and rulings›.

Times Wherein Prayer is Prohibited

وَأَوْقَاتُ اَلنَّهْيِ خَمْسَةٌ: مِنْ طُلُوعِ فَجْرٍ ثَانٍ إِلَى طُلُوعِ اَلشَّمْسِ، وَمِنْ صَلَاةِ اَلْعَصْرِ إِلَى اَلْغُرُوبِ، وَعِنْدَ طُلُوعِهَا إِلَى اِرْتِفَاعِهَا قَدْرَ رُمْحٍ، وَعِنْدَ قِيَامِهَا حَتَّى تَزُولَ وَعِنْدَ غُرُوبِهَا حَتَّى يَتِمَّ.

فَيَحْرُمُ اِبْتِدَاءُ نَفْلٍ فِيهَا مُطْلَقًا لَا قَضَاءُ فَرْضٍ، وَفِعْلُ رَكْعَتَيْ طَوَافٍ، وَسُنَّةُ فَجْرٍ أَدَاءً قَبْلَهَا، وَصَلَاةُ جِنَازَةٍ بَعْدَ فَجْرٍ وَعَصْرٍ.

The times wherein prayer is prohibited are five:

‹1› from the beginning of true sunrise until the sun has risen;

‹2› after praying Midafternoon Prayer [*ʿaṣr*] until the sun has set;

‹3› from sunrise until the sun has risen a spear's length [above the horizon];

‹4› from its zenith until it starts to descend; and,

‹5› when the sun begins to set until it has completely set.

So it is unlawful to begin a voluntary prayer during those times, whatever the circumstances [*muṭlaqan*] [whether one knows, forgets, or is ignorant; one sins if one is in the midst of a voluntary prayer when one of these times enters]. But it is not unlawful to make up a missed obligatory [*farḍ*] prayer, to perform the two prayer-cycles for Circumambulation or the two recommended to be performed before Dawn Prayer, or the Funeral Prayer after Dawn or Midafternoon Prayers.

Congregational Prayer

(فَصْلٌ) تَجِبُ اَلْجَمَاعَةُ لِلْخَمْسِ اَلْمُؤَدَّاةِ عَلَى اَلرِّجَالِ اَلْأَحْرَارِ اَلْقَادِرِينَ، وَحَرُمَ أَنْ يُؤَمَّ قَبْلَ رَاتِبٍ إِلَّا بِإِذْنِهِ، أَوْ عُذْرِهِ، أَوْ عَدَمِ كَرَاهَتِهِ.

Praying in a congregation is obligatory for current performances of the five daily prayers for men who are free and able.

It is unlawful to lead a prayer before the assigned imam has done so – unless one has the imam's permission ‹if the assigned imam dislikes this›, he is excused ‹if the imam is late and the time has become restricted›, or the imam does not dislike it.

وَمَنْ كَبَّرَ قَبْلَ تَسْلِيمَةِ اَلْإِمَامِ اَلْأُولَى أَدْرَكَ اَلْجَمَاعَةَ، وَمَنْ أَدْرَكَهُ رَاكِعًا أَدْرَكَ رَكْعَةً، بِشَرْطِ إِدْرَاكِهِ رَاكِعًا، وَعَدَمِ شَكِّهِ فِيهِ، وتحريمته قَائِمًا.

وَتُسَنُّ ثَانِيَةٌ لِلرُّكُوعِ، وَمَا أَدْرَكَ مَعَهُ آخِرُهَا، وَمَا يَقْضِيهِ أَوَّلُهَا.

Whoever makes an initial "*Allāhu akbar*" before the imam's final "*as-salāmu ʿalaykum*" has caught the congregational prayer.

Whoever catches [up with] the imam while he is bowing has caught the prayer-cycle – provided that one catches him mid-bow without having any doubt about it and that one makes one's inaugural "*Allāhu akbar*" while standing. It is recommended that one make a second "*Allāhu akbar*" for bowing.

Whatever [part of the prayer a latecomer] catches with the imam is from the end of one's prayer. Whatever one makes up is from its beginning.

وَيَتَحَمَّلُ عَنْ مَأْمُومٍ قِرَاءَةً، وَسُجُودَ سَهْوٍ وَتِلَاوَةٍ، وَسُتْرَةً وَدُعَاءَ قُنُوتٍ، وَتَشَهُّدًا أَوَّلَ إِذَا سُبِقَ بِرَكْعَةٍ، لَكِنْ يُسَنُّ أَنْ يَقْرَأَ فِي سَكَتَاتِهِ وَسِرِّيَّةٍ، وَإِذَا لَمْ يَسْمَعْهُ لِبُعْدٍ لَا طَرَشٍ.

The imam assumes responsibility for the recitation [of Al-Fātiḥah], the prostrations of forgetfulness and recitation, the barrier [*sutrah*] [since the imam's barrier is a barrier for whoever is behind him], the *Qunūt* supplication, and the first *tashahhud* ‹of a four-prayer-cycle prayer› when the follower is late by one prayer-cycle ‹since following the imam is obligatory›. However, it is recommended for the follower to recite when the imam pauses or recites inaudibly, and when the follower cannot hear him due to being distant – but not due to deafness.

وَسُنَّ لَهُ اَلتَّخْفِيفُ مَعَ اَلْإِتْمَامِ، وَتَطْوِيلُ اَلْأُولَى عَلَى اَلثَّانِيَةِ، وَانْتِظَارُ دَاخِلٍ مَا لَمْ يَشُقَّ.

The imam is recommended to be brief while being complete, to lengthen the first prayer-cycle over the second, and to wait for an entrant so long as it is not difficult to do so.

Imams

(فَصْلٌ) اَلْأَقْرَأُ اَلْعَالِمُ فِقْهَ صَلَاتِهِ أَوْلَى مِنْ اَلْأَفْقَهِ، وَلَا تَصِحُّ خَلْفَ فَاسِقٍ إِلَّا فِي جُمُعَةٍ وَعِيدٍ تَعَذُّرًا خَلْفَ غَيْرِهِ، وَلَا إِمَامَةُ مَنْ حَدَثُهُ دَائِمٌ وَأُمِّيٌّ وَهُوَ مَنْ لَا يُحْسِنُ اَلْفَاتِحَةَ، أَوْ يُدْغِمُ فِيهَا حَرْفًا لَا يُدْغَمُ أَوْ يَلْحَنُ (فِيهَا) لَحْنًا يُحِيلُ اَلْمَعْنَى إِلَّا بِمِثْلِهِ.

An expert reciter who knows the fiqh of his prayer is superior ‹for leading prayers› to one more knowledgeable in fiqh ‹but who is not good with recitation›.

Prayer is not valid behind someone who is immoral (except for Friday and Eid Prayers that one cannot pray behind someone else). Neither is being led by someone who is in a perpetual state of ritual impurity, or someone illiterate (‹in popular convention:› someone who does not read Al-Fātiḥah correctly, nasalizes [makes *idghām* of] a letter that should not be, or mispronounces letters in a way that corrupts the meaning) – unless the follower is like him.

وَكَذَا مَنْ بِهِ سَلَسُ بَوْلٍ وَعَاجِزٍ عَنْ رُكُوعٍ وَسُجُودٍ، أَوْ قُعُودٍ وَنَحْوِهَا، أَوْ اِجْتِنَابِ نَجَاسَةٍ أَوْ اِسْتِقْبَالٍ، وَلَا عَاجِزٍ عَنْ قِيَامٍ بِقَادِرٍ إِلَّا رَاتِبًا رُجِيَ زَوَالُ عِلَّتِهِ، وَلَا مُمَيِّزٍ لِبَالِغٍ فِي فَرْضٍ، وَلَا اِمْرَأَةٍ لِرِجَالٍ وَخُنَاثٍ وَلَا خَلْفَ مُحْدِثٍ أَوْ نَجِسٍ، فَإِنْ جَهِلَا حَتَّى اِنْقَضَتْ صَحَّتْ لِمَأْمُومٍ، وَتُكْرَهُ إِمَامَةُ لَحَّانٍ وَفَأْفَاءٍ وَنَحْوِهِ.

One also cannot follow an imam who is incontinent; cannot bow, prostrate, sit, or the like ‹e.g., like rising – unless their conditions are identical›; or ‹cannot fulfill a condition, such as someone› who cannot avoid filth or face the direction of prayer.

Someone who can stand cannot follow an imam who cannot stand – unless the imam is the mosque's official imam and his problem is expected to get better.

Someone who is mature cannot pray an obligatory [*farḍ*] prayer behind someone who [just] has discernment. ‹But his leadership is valid in voluntary prayers and when leading his like.›

A man cannot follow a woman or a hermaphrodite.

‹There is no difference here between obligatory and voluntary prayers. But *Al-Muntahā* and its commentary say: "Except most of the early scholars [say that] if they – meaning women and hermaphrodites – recite correctly while the men are illiterate. In that case, their leadership is valid – but only in Tarawih – and they stand behind the men."[2]›

One cannot pray behind an imam who has ritual impurity ‹who knows that he has minor or major ritual impurity› or ‹inexcusable› filth ‹on his body, garment, or place of prayer›. If the two are unaware until finishing the prayer, the prayer is valid for the follower.

---

2. See al-Buhūtī *Sharḥ Muntahā al-Irādāt,* 1:275; and his *Kashshāf al-Qināʿ*, 1:479.

The leadership [in prayer] of someone who replaces letters or stutters is offensive ‹though valid›.

وَسُنَّ وُقُوفُ ٱلْمَأْمُومِينَ خَلْفَ ٱلْإِمَامِ، وَالْوَاحِدُ عَنْ يَمِينِهِ وُجُوبًا، وَالْمَرْأَةُ خَلْفَهُ، وَمَنْ صَلَّى عَنْ يَسَارِ ٱلْإِمَامِ مَعَ خُلُوِّ يَمِينِهِ أَوْ فَذًّا رَكْعَةً لَمْ تَصِحَّ صَلَاتُهُ، فَإِذَا جَمَعَهُمَا مَسْجِدٌ صَحَّتْ ٱلْقُدْوَةُ مُطْلَقًا، بِشَرْطِ ٱلْعِلْمِ بِانْتِقَالَاتِ ٱلْإِمَامِ وَإِلَّا شُرِطَ رُؤْيَةُ ٱلْإِمَامِ أَوْ مَنْ وَرَاءَهُ أَيْضًا، وَلَوْ فِي بَعْضِهَا.

It is recommended for followers to stand behind the imam. It is obligatory for a single follower to stand to the imam's right, and for a female to stand behind a male imam. The prayer of the follower is invalid if the follower prays to left of the imam while the right is empty, or prays a ‹complete› prayer-cycle alone ‹even when it is a single woman praying behind another woman› in the line [except when a lone female follower prays behind a male imam]. ‹If someone leads a man and a woman in prayer, the man stands to his right and the woman behind him.›

If an imam and a follower are in the same mosque, following is valid – categorically [*muṭlaqan*] ‹i.e., whether the follower sees the imam, whether people behind him see him›, provided that there is knowledge of the imam's transitions ‹by hearing the sayings of "*Allāhu akbar*"›. Otherwise, ‹if they are not in the same mosque by both or one of them being outside the mosque – or even in another mosque,› seeing the imam (or also whoever is behind him) is a condition – even if only for part of the prayer.

وَكُرِهَ عُلُوُّ إِمَامٍ عَلَى مَأْمُومٍ ذِرَاعًا فَأَكْثَرَ، وَصَلَاتُهُ فِي مِحْرَابٍ يَمْنَعُ مُشَاهَدَتَهُ، وَتَطَوُّعُهُ مَوْضِعَ ٱلْمَكْتُوبَةِ، وَإِطَالَتُهُ ٱلِاسْتِقْبَالَ بَعْدَ ٱلسَّلَامِ، وَوُقُوفُ مَأْمُومٍ بَيْنَ سَوَارٍ تَقْطَعُ ٱلصُّفُوفَ عُرْفًا إِلَّا لِحَاجَةٍ فِي ٱلْكُلِّ، وَحُضُورُ مَسْجِدٍ وَجَمَاعَةٍ لِمَنْ رَائِحَتُهُ كَرِيهَةٌ مِنْ بَصَلٍ أَوْ غَيْرِهِ.

It is offensive for an imam to be higher than a follower by one *dhirāʿ* [32 centimeter/12.6 inches] or more; to pray in a prayer niche [*miḥrāb*] that prevents him being seen ‹by followers›; to pray a voluntary prayer where he ‹had just› prayed an obligatory prayer; and to face the direction of prayer for a long time after giving the closing "*as-salāmu ʿalaykum*" ‹in the absence of women or some need to do so. If he does prolong his sitting, followers can depart. If he does not prolong, it is recommended for followers to not depart before the imam›.

‹It is offensive› for followers to stand, without need, between pillars that are customarily considered to interrupt the lines.

All [of the above are offensive] unless there is a need ‹like the mosque becoming constricted due to a large congregation›.

‹It is offensive for› someone with offensive odors, such as from onions or something else ‹like garlic, leek or radish; and like underarm odor, leprosy, bad breath›, to attend the mosque and congregational prayer.

وَيُعْذَرُ بِتَرْكِ جُمُعَةٍ وَجَمَاعَةٍ مَرِيضٌ، وَمُدَافِعُ أَحَدِ الْأَخْبَثَيْنِ وَمَنْ بِحَضْرَةِ طَعَامٍ يَحْتَاجُ إِلَيْهِ، وَخَائِفٌ ضَيَاعَ مَالِهِأَوْ مَوْتَ قَرِيبِهِ أَوْ ضَرَرًا مِنْ سُلْطَانٍ أَوْ مَطَرٍ وَنَحْوِهِ، أَوْ مُلَازَمَةَ غَرِيمٍ وَلَا وَفَاءَ لَهُ، أَوْ فَوْتَ رُفْقَتِهِ وَنَحْوِهِمْ.

One is excused from attending Friday Prayer and congregational prayer when one is sick; has pressing need to relieve himself of urine or feces; is in the presence of food one needs; fears that one's property will be misplaced; fears the death of a relative; fears harm to oneself from the authorities, rain, or the like ‹e.g., a predatory beast, a robber›; fears a debt collector while one cannot fulfill the debt; fears missing one's travel companions or the like ‹e.g., intense drowsiness leading one to fear missing the prayer in its time›.

People Who Have Excuses

(فَصْلٌ) يُصَلِّي ٱلْمَرِيضُ قَائِمًا، فَإِنْ لَمْ يَسْتَطِعْ فَقَاعِدًا، فَإِنْ لَمْ يَسْتَطِعْ فَعَلَى جَنْبٍ، وَالْأَيْمَنُ أَفْضَلُ، وَكُرِهَ مُسْتَلْقِيًا مَعَ قُدْرَتِهِ عَلَى جَنْبٍ وَإِلَّا تَعَيَّنَ، وَيُومِئُ بِرُكُوعٍ وَسُجُودٍ وَيَجْعَلُهُ أَخْفَضَ، فَإِنْ عَجَزَ أَوْمَأَ بِطَرْفِهِ وَنَوَى بِقَلْبِهِ كَأَسِيرٍ خَائِفٍ، فَإِنْ عَجَزَ فَبِقَلْبِهِ مُسْتَحْضِرَ ٱلْقَوْلِ وَالْفِعْلِ، وَلَا يَسْقُطُ فِعْلُهَا مَا دَامَ ٱلْعَقْلُ ثَابِتًا، فَإِنْ طَرَأَ عَجْزٌ أَوْ قُدْرَةٌ فِي أَثْنَائِهَا ٱنْتَقَلَ وَبَنَى.

Someone sick prays standing if he can. If unable ‹to pray standing›, then one prays seated. If one is not able ‹to pray seated or it is difficult›, then ‹lying› on one's side (with the right being best). It is offensive to pray lying on one's back when one can pray on the side – otherwise [if unable to pray on one's side], then it is required ‹that one pray on one's back with the feet towards the direction of prayer›.

Someone ‹who cannot bow or prostrate› nods in place of bowing and prostrating, and makes a deeper nod for the prostration. If one is unable ‹to nod with one's head›, one gestures with the eyes and intends it with the heart – like a fearful prisoner. If one is unable ‹to gesture with the eyes›, then one does it in one's heart, bringing the utterance and actions into mind.

Its performance never ceases being obligatory so long as one's intellect remains.

If one becomes unable or able in the midst of prayer, one switches and continues his prayer.

Travel and Peril

(فَصْلٌ) وَيُسَنُّ قَصْرُ ٱلرُّبَاعِيَّةِ فِي سَفَرٍ طَوِيلٍ مُبَاحٍ وَيَقْضِي صَلَاةَ سَفَرٍ فِي حَضَرٍ وَعَكْسُهُ تَامَّةً.

It is recommended to shorten four-prayer-cycle prayers during a lawful long journey. A prayer missed during a journey that is made up while resident (and the opposite) is made up in its full form.

وَمَنْ نَوَى إِقَامَةً مُطْلَقَةً بِمَوْضِعٍ، أَوْ أَكْثَرَ مِنْ أَرْبَعَةِ أَيَّامٍ، أَوْ ائْتَمَّ بِمُقِيمٍ أَتَمَّ، وَإِنْ حُبِسَ ظُلْمًا، أَوْ لَمْ يَنْوِ إِقَامَةً قَصَرَ أَبَدًا وَيُبَاحُ لَهُ اَلْجَمْعُ بَيْنَ اَلظُّهْرَيْنِ وَالْعِشَائَيْنِ بِوَقْتِ إِحْدَاهُمَا.

One prays the full form if: one intends to reside in a location categorically [*muṭlaqan*] ‹i.e., without qualifying its time› or for more than four days; or prays behind someone praying the full form. One can shorten [prayers] indefinitely if they are unjustly imprisoned, or did not plan to reside.

It is permissible for one ‹without it being offensive or recommended, though it is best to omit› to combine the Noon and Afternoon Prayers, and the Sunset and Night Prayers, in the time of either one of them.

وَلِمَرِيضٍ وَنَحْوِهِ يَلْحَقُهُ بِتَرْكِهِ مَشَقَّةٌ وَبَيْنَ الْعِشَائَيْنِ فَقَطْ لِمَطَرٍ وَنَحْوِهِ يَبُلُّ اَلثَّوْبَ، وَتُوجَدُ مَعَهُ مَشَقَّةٌ، وَلِوَحْلٍ وَرِيحٍ شَدِيدَةٍ بَارِدَةٍ لَا بَارِدَةٍ فَقَطْ، إِلَّا بِلَيْلَةٍ مُظْلِمَةٍ.

‹Shortening is permissible in eight situations. The first is during travel. The second is› someone who is sick or the like who would suffer a hardship if he does not combine prayers. ‹[The rest – with slight abridgment – are:] nursing, due frequent filth, irregular bleeding, someone who cannot make purification or dry ablution for each prayer, someone who cannot know the time (like someone who is blind), someone who has an excuse to not pray with a congregation or Friday Prayer (like someone fearing for his life, property, or wife), someone busy with something excusing him from attending the above (like someone who fears harm to their needed livelihood.›

It is permissible to combine only the Sunset and Night Prayers due to rain and the like ‹e.g., snow, hail, ice› that wets the garment and involves hardship. It is also permissible due to mud and fierce cold wind (not just cold wind, except during a dark night [night is the author's preference]).

وَالْأَفْضَلُ فِعْلُ ٱلْأَرْفَقِ مِنْ تَقْدِيمٍ أَوْ تَأْخِيرٍ، وَكُرِهَ فِعْلُهُ فِي بَيْتِهِ وَنَحْوِهِ بِلَا ضَرُورَةٍ وَيَبْطُلُ جَمْعُ تَقْدِيمٍ بِرَاتِبَةٍ بَيْنَهُمَا، وَتَفْرِيقٍ بِأَكْثَرَ مِنْ وُضُوءٍ خَفِيفٍ وَإِقَامَةٍ.

It is best to do whichever is most convenient: praying both in the first time, or delaying to the second.

It is offensive to combine inside one's own house without necessity.

Praying in the first time is invalidated if a voluntary prayer associated with the obligatory prayer [*rātibah*] is prayed between the obligatory prayers; and if they are separated by more than the time needed to make a brief ablution and the call to commence the prayer.

وَتَجُوزُ صَلَاةُ ٱلْخَوْفِ بِأَيِّ صِفَةٍ صَحَّتْ عَنِ ٱلنَّبِيِّ ﷺ وَصَحَّتْ عَنْ سِتَّةِ أَوْجُهٍ وَسُنَّ فِيهَا حَمْلُ سِلَاحٍ غَيْرِ مُثْقِلٍ.

It is permissible to pray the Prayer of Peril in any way that is authentically transmitted from the Prophet ﷺ. Six manners are authentic. It is recommended to carry light weapons during the Prayer of Peril.

Friday Prayer

(فَصْلٌ) تَلْزَمُ ٱلْجُمُعَةُ كُلَّ مُسْلِمٍ مُكَلَّفٍ ذَكَرٍ حُرٍّ مُسْتَوْطِنٍ بِبِنَاءٍ.

Friday Prayer is required of every Muslim who is responsible, male, free, and resident in a place with built structures.

وَمَنْ صَلَّى ٱلظُّهْرَ مِمَّنْ عَلَيْهِ ٱلْجُمُعَةُ قَبْلَ ٱلْإِمَامِ لَمْ تَصِحَّ، وَإِلَّا صَحَّتْ وَٱلْأَفْضَلُ بَعْدَهُ، وَحَرُمَ سَفَرُ مَنْ تَلْزَمُهُ بَعْدَ ٱلزَّوَالِ وَكُرِهَ قَبْلَهُ مَا لَمْ يَأْتِ بِهَا فِي طَرِيقِهِ أَوْ يَخَفْ فَوْتَ رُفْقَةٍ.

It is not valid if someone who must pray the Friday Prayer prays the Noon Prayer before the imam ‹prays›. But if one's attendance is not obligatory, it is valid ‹to pray it before the imam's prayer›, though afterwards is best.

It is unlawful for someone who is required to attend Friday Prayer to travel after the sun passes its zenith [until after he prays]. It is offensive to travel before when one does not pray it along the way or does not fear missing his traveling companions.

وَشُرِطَ لِصِحَّتِهَا اَلْوَقْتُ، وَهُوَ أَوَّلُ وَقْتِ اَلْعِيدِ إِلَى آخِرِ وَقْتِ اَلظُّهْرِ، فَإِنْ خَرَجَ قَبْلَ التحريمة صَلَّوْا ظُهْرًا وَإِلَّا جُمُعَةً، وَحُضُورُ أَرْبَعِينَ بِالْإِمَامِ مِنْ أَهْلِ وُجُوبِهَا فَإِنْ نَقَصُوا قَبْلَ إِتْمَامِهَا اِسْتَأْنَفُوا جُمُعَةً إِنْ أَمْكَنَ وَإِلَّا ظُهْرًا، وَمَنْ أَدْرَكَ مَعَ اَلْإِمَامِ رَكْعَةً أَتَمَّهَا جُمُعَةً.

Conditions for its validity include its time, which is from the start of the time for Eid ‹the sun rising a spear's length above the horizon› until the end of Noon Prayer. If the time exits before making the initial "*Allāhu akbar,*" they pray Noon Prayer. Otherwise, they pray Friday Prayer.

[The conditions for its validity include] the attendance of forty (including the imam) who are required to attend. If they fall short before finishing it, they continue it as Friday Prayer if possible. Otherwise, they finish it as Noon Prayer.

Whoever prays one prayer-cycle with the imam finishes it as Friday Prayer. ‹Otherwise, he prays it as Noon Prayer if its time has entered.›

وَتَقْدِيمُ خُطْبَتَيْنِ مِنْ شَرْطِهِمَا: اَلْوَقْتُ، وَحَمْدُ اَللهِ، وَالصَّلَاةُ عَلَى رَسُولِهِ -عَلَيْهِ اَلسَّلَامُ-، وَقِرَاءَةُ آيَةٍ، وَحُضُورُ اَلْعَدَدِ اَلْمُعْتَبَرِ، وَرَفْعُ اَلصَّوْتِ بِقَدْرِ إِسْمَاعِهِ، وَالنِّيَّةُ، وَالْوَصِيَّةُ بِتَقْوَى اَللهِ، وَلَا يَتَعَيَّنُ لَفْظُهَا، وَأَنْ تَكُونَا مِمَّنْ يَصِحُّ أَنْ يَؤُمَّ فِيهَا لَا مِمَّنْ يَتَوَلَّى اَلصَّلَاةَ.

[The conditions for its validity include] it being preceded by two sermons. The conditions of the sermons include: the time; praising Allah ‹with the phrase "*Al-Ḥamdu li-Llāh*"›; prayers upon the Messenger of Allah ﷺ ‹with the phrase "*al-ṣalāt*"›; reciting a verse of the Quran; the significant number attending; raising the voice so it is heard ‹by the required number›; intention; advising fear of Allah – and its phrase is not specified; being delivered by someone who could lead a valid Friday Prayer – though not [necessarily] the one who does lead the prayer.

وَتُسَنُّ اَلْخُطْبَةُ عَلَى مِنْبَرٍ أَوْ مَوْضِعٍ عَالٍ، وَسَلَامُ خَطِيبٍ إِذَا خَرَجَ، وَإِذَا أَقْبَلَ عَلَيْهِمْ وَجُلُوسُهُ إِلَى فَرَاغِ اَلْأَذَانِ، وَبَيْنَهُمَا قَلِيلًا، وَالْخُطْبَةُ قَائِمًا مُعْتَمِدًا عَلَى سَيْفٍ أَوْ عَصًا قَاصِدًا تِلْقَاءَهُ، وَتَقْصِيرُهُمَا، وَالثَّانِيَةُ أَقْصَرُ، وَالدُّعَاءُ لِلْمُسْلِمِينَ، وَأُبِيحَ لِمُعَيَّنٍ كَالسُّلْطَانِ.

It is recommended for the sermon to be from a *minbar* or a platform; to say "*as-salāmu ʿalaykum*" going out ‹to the congregants› and when he faces them; to sit until the Call to Prayer [*adhān*] is finished; to sit shortly between the two sermons; to deliver the sermon standing while leaning upon a sword or staff; to make eye contact; to keep the sermons brief – with the second shorter than the first; to supplicate for Muslims in general – with it being permissible to supplicate for a specific individual, like the governor.

وَهِيَ رَكْعَتَانِ يَقْرَأُ فِي اَلْأُولَى بَعْدَ اَلْفَاتِحَةِ اَلْجُمُعَةَ وَالثَّانِيَةِ اَلْمُنَافِقِينَ. وَحَرُمَ إِقَامَتُهَا وَعِيدٍ فِي أَكْثَرَ مِنْ مَوْضِعٍ بِبَلَدٍ إِلَّا لِحَاجَةٍ.

The Friday Prayer is two prayer-cycles. After Al-Fātiḥah [Q1], in the first prayer-cycle, ‹it is recommended that› one reads Al-Jumuʿah [Q62], and in the second Al-Munāfiqīn [Q63].

It is unlawful to hold Friday and Eid Prayers in multiple locations within a single land unless there is a need to do so ‹e.g., due to the mosque being too small, distance, fear of discord (*fitnah*)›.

وَأَقَلُّ اَلسُّنَّةِ بَعْدَهَا رَكْعَتَانِ وَأَكْثَرُهَا سِتٌّ. وَسُنَّ قَبْلَهَا أَرْبَعٌ غَيْرُ رَاتِبَةٍ، وَقِرَاءَةُ اَلْكَهْفِ فِي يَوْمِهَا وَلَيْلَتِهَا،

The minimum recommended prayer after it is two prayer-cycles; the maximum is six.

It is recommended to pray four prayer-cycles before it – though they are not associated with it [*rātibah*]; and to recite Al-Kahf [Q18] during its night and ‹also during its› day.

وَكَثْرَةُ دُعَاءٍ وَصَلَاةٍ على اَلنَّبِيِّ ﷺ وَغُسْلٌ وتنظفٌ وتَطَيّبٌ وَلبسُ بَيْضَاءَ وَتَبْكِيرٌ إِلَيْهَا مَاشِيًا وَدنوٌّ مِنَ الإِمَامِ.

‹It is recommended› to supplicate abundantly; to make ‹numerous› prayers upon the Prophet ﷺ; to wash, cleanse, use scent, and wear white; to go early, walking; and to be close to the imam.

وَكُرِهَ لِغَيْرِهِ تَخَطِّي اَلرِّقَابِ إِلَّا لِفُرْجَةٍ لَا يَصِلُ إِلَيْهَا إِلَّا بِهِ، وَإِيثَارٌ بِمَكَانٍ أَفْضَلَ لَا قَبُولٌ.

وَحَرُمَ أَنْ يُقِيمَ غَيْرَ صَبِيٍّ مِنْ مَكَانِهِ فَيَجْلِسُ فِيهِ، وَالْكَلَامُ حَالَ اَلْخُطْبَةِ عَلَى غَيْرِ خَطِيبٍ، وَمَنْ كَلَّمَهُ لِحَاجَةٍ، وَمَنْ دَخَلَ -وَالإِمَامُ يَخْطُبُ- صَلَّى اَلتَّحِيَّةَ فَقَط خَفِيفَةً.

It is offensive for someone other than the imam to step over others – unless to reach an empty spot unreachable without stepping over them.

It is offensive to offer a superior place to someone else (though it is not offensive to accept it).

It is unlawful to move someone who is not a child to sit in his spot; for someone other than the *khaṭīb* to speak during the sermon; or for someone to speak to the *khaṭīb* out of need.

Whoever enters while the *khatīb* is delivering the sermon prays only the Greeting Prayer, briefly.

Eid Prayer

(فَصْلٌ) وَصَلَاةُ اَلْعِيدَيْنِ فَرْضُ كِفَايَةٍ، وَوَقْتُهَا كَصَلَاةِ اَلضُّحَى وَآخِرُهُ اَلزَّوَالُ.
فَإِنْ لَمْ يُعْلَمْ بِالْعِيدِ إِلَّا بَعْدَهُ صَلَّوْا مِنْ اَلْغَدِ قَضَاءً.

Praying the two Eid Prayers is a communal obligation [*farḍ*]. Its time is the same as Ḍuḥā Prayer ‹i.e., once the sun has risen a spear's length above the horizon›; it ends when the sun reaches its zenith. If Eid is not known until it has passed, they pray it the next day as a makeup prayer.

وَشُرِطَ لِوُجُوبِهَا شُرُوطُ جُمُعَةٍ، وَلِصِحَّتِهَا اِسْتِيطَانٌ، وَعَدَدُ اَلْجُمُعَةِ، لَكِنْ يُسَنُّ لِمَنْ
فَاتَتْهُ أَوْ بِبَعْضِهَا أَنْ يَقْضِيَهَا، وَعَلَى صِفَتِهَا أَفْضَلُ.

The conditions for it being obligatory are the same as the conditions for Friday Prayer.

The conditions for its validity include permanent residency [for the required number of attendees] and the number for the Friday Prayer. ‹The Imam's permission is not required.› However, it is recommended for whoever missed the Eid Prayer (or part of it) to make it up, and doing it according to its [special] characteristics is superior.

‹There is no harm for women who have not perfumed or adorned themselves to attend, apart from the men. Women during menses sit apart from the place of prayer but where they can hear.›

وَتُسَنُّ فِي صَحْرَاءَ، وَتَأْخِيرُ صَلَاةِ فِطْرٍ، وَأَكْلٌ قَبْلَهَا، وَتَقْدِيمُ أَضْحَى، وَتَرْكُ أَكْلٍ
قَبْلَهَا لِمُضَحٍّ.

It is recommended to be performed in a vacant area [*ṣaḥrā'*].

‹It is recommended for› the prayer for Eid al-Fiṭr to be delayed and to eat beforehand.

‹It is recommended for› the prayer for Eid al-Aḍḥā to be early and for someone who will be sacrificing not to eat before the prayer.

وَيُصَلِّيهَا رَكْعَتَيْنِ قَبْلَ اَلْخُطْبَةِ، يُكَبِّرُ فِي اَلْأُولَى بَعْدَ اَلِاسْتِفْتَاحِ، وَقَبْلَ اَلتَّعَوُّذِ وَالْقِرَاءَةِ سِتًّا، وَفِي اَلثَّانِيَةِ قَبْلَ اَلْقِرَاءَةِ خَمْسًا، رَافِعًا يَدَهُ مَعَ كُلِّ تَكْبِيرَةٍ، وَيَقُولُ بَيْنَ كُلِّ تَكْبِيرَتَيْنِ: «اَللهُ أَكْبَرُ كَبِيرًا، وَالْحَمْدُ للهِ كَثِيرًا، وَسُبْحَانَ اَللهِ بُكْرَةً وَأَصِيلاً، وَصَلَّى اَللهُ عَلَى مُحَمَّدٍ وَآلِهِ وَسَلَّمَ تَسْلِيمًا كَثِيرًا» أَوْ غَيْرَهُ، ثُمَّ يَقْرَأُ بَعْدَ اَلْفَاتِحَةِ فِي اَلْأُولَى «سَبِّحْ» وَالثَّانِيَةِ «اَلْغَاشِيَةَ»، ثُمَّ يَخْطُبُ كَخُطْبَتَيِ اَلْجُمُعَةِ لَكِنْ يَسْتَفْتِحُ فِي اَلْأُولَى بِتِسْعِ تَكْبِيرَاتٍ وَالثَّانِيَةَ بِسَبْعٍ، وَيُبَيِّنُ لَهُمْ فِي اَلْفِطْرِ مَا يُخْرِجُونَ وَفِي اَلْأَضْحَى مَا يُضَحُّونَ.

One prays Eid Prayer as two prayer-cycles before the sermon. After the opening supplication, but before seeking protection from Satan and recitation, one says *"Allāhu akbar"* six times. In the second, before recitation, one says *"Allāhu akbar"* five times. One raises the hands with each saying of *"Allāhu akbar,"* and between each pair one says, *"Allāhu akbar kabīran wa l-ḥamdu li-Llāhi kathīran wa subḥāna Llāhi bukratan wa aṣīlan wa ṣalla Llāhu ʿalā Muḥammadin wa ālihi wa sallim taslīman kathīran"* ("Allah is ever greatest. Much praise be to Allah. Glory to Him, morning and evening. And may the prayers of Allah be upon Muḥammad and upon his household, and plentiful peace") or something else. After Al-Fātiḥah [Q1], in the first prayer-cycle one reads Al-Aʿlā [Q87], and in the second Al-Ghāshiyah [Q88]. Then, ‹when the *khaṭīb* finishes the prayer, he› delivers a sermon like the two sermons of Friday Prayer. However, he begins the first with nine sayings of *"Allāhu akbar,"* and the second with seven. During Eid al-Fiṭr, he clarifies what they must pay ‹for *zakāt al-fiṭr*›; and during Eid al-Aḍḥā ‹he clarifies› what they sacrifice.

وَسُنَّ اَلتَّكْبِيرُ اَلْمُطْلَقُ لَيْلَتَيِ اَلْعِيدِ، وَالْفِطْرُ آكَدُ، وَمِنْ أَوَّلِ ذِي اَلْحِجَّةِ إِلَى فَرَاغِ اَلْخُطْبَةِ، وَالْمُقَيَّدُ عَقِبَ كُلِّ فَرِيضَةٍ فِي جَمَاعَةٍ مِنْ فَجْرِ عَرَفَةَ لِمُحِلٍّ وَلِمُحْرِمٍ مِنْ ظُهْرِ يَوْمِ اَلنَّحْرِ إِلَى عَصْرِ آخِرِ أَيَّامِ اَلتَّشْرِيقِ.

It is recommended to make the unrestricted *takbīr* [*al-takbīr al-muṭlaq*] on the nights before both Eids, with it being more emphatic for Eid al-Fiṭr; and from the beginning of ‹the tenth of› Dhi l-Ḥijjah until finishing the sermon.

‹It is recommended› to make the restricted *takbīr* [*al-takbīr al-muqayyad*] after every obligatory prayer performed in a congregation, starting at Dawn Prayer on the day of ʿArafah [9 Dhi l-Ḥijjah] for non-pilgrims and Noon Prayer on the Day of Sacrifices [10 Dhi l-Ḥijjah] for pilgrims, up until Midafternoon Prayer on the last of the Days of Tashrīq [11–13 Dhi l-Ḥijjah].

Eclipse & Drought Prayers

(فَصْلٌ) وَتُسَنُّ صَلَاةُ كُسُوفٍ رَكْعَتَيْنِ، كُلُّ رَكْعَةٍ بِقِيَامَيْنِ وَرُكُوعَيْنِ، وَتَطْوِيلُ سُورَةٍ وَتَسْبِيحٍ، وَكَوْنُ أَوَّلِ كُلٍّ أَطْوَلَ، وَاسْتِسْقَاءٍ إِذَا أَجْدَبَتِ ٱلْأَرْضُ وَقُحِطَ ٱلْمَطَرُ.

وَصِفَتُهَا وَأَحْكَامُهَا كَعِيدٍ، وَهِيَ وَٱلَّتِي قَبْلَهَا جَمَاعَةً أَفْضَلُ.

It is recommended to pray the Eclipse Prayer as two prayer-cycles. Each prayer-cycle has two standings and bowings, with prolonged recitation and invocations during the bowing and prostration – with the first prayer-cycle being longer.

‹It is recommended to pray› the Drought Prayer when lands ‹– even elsewhere –› become barren, and when there is a drought. Its description and rulings are like Eid. Praying it and the one before it ‹i.e., the Eclipse Prayer› in congregation is superior ‹to praying it alone›.

وَإِذَا أَرَادَ ٱلْإِمَامُ ٱلْخُرُوجَ لَهَا وَعَظَ ٱلنَّاسَ، وَأَمَرَهُمْ بِالتَّوْبَةِ، وَالْخُرُوجِ مِنَ ٱلْمَظَالِمِ، وَتَرْكِ ٱلتَّشَاحُنِ وَالصِّيَامِ وَالصَّدَقَةِ، وَيَعِدُهُمْ يَوْمًا يَخْرُجُونَ فِيهِ، وَيَخْرُجُ مُتَوَاضِعًا مُتَخَشِّعًا مُتَذَلِّلًا مُتَضَرِّعًا مُتَنَظِّفًا لَا مُطَيَّبًا، وَمَعَهُ أَهْلُ ٱلدِّينِ وَالصَّلَاحِ وَالشُّيُوخُ، وَمُمَيِّزُ ٱلصِّبْيَانِ، فَيُصَلِّي ثُمَّ يَخْطُبُ وَاحِدَةً يَفْتَتِحُهَا بِالتَّكْبِيرِ كَخُطْبَةِ عِيدٍ، وَيُكْثِرُ فِيهَا

اَلاِسْتِغْفَارَ، وَقِرَاءَةَ اَلْآيَاتِ اَلَّتِي فِيهَا اَلْأَمْرُ بِهِ، وَيَرْفَعُ يَدَيْهِ وَظُهُورُهُمَا نَحْوَ اَلسَّمَاءِ فَيَدْعُو بِدُعَاءِ اَلنَّبِيِّ ﷺ وَمِنْهُ: «اَللَّهُمَّ اِسْقِنَا غَيْثًا مُغِيثًا» إِلَى آخِرِهِ.

When the Imam intends to go out for it, he exhorts the masses and commands them to repent, to return anything taken unjustly, to forsake enmity, to fast, and to give charity. He appoints a day for them to go out. They go out humbly ‹wearing their work clothes›, with humility, meekness, and tranquility. They go out clean ‹having washed, pared their nails, and removed offensive smells› but without applying perfume.

The Imam goes out with the religious, righteous, elderly, and youths who are discerning [*mumayyiz*].

The Imam prays and then gives a single sermon. He begins it with saying "*Allāhu akbar*" as with an Eid sermon. During the sermon, he frequently asks for forgiveness and recites verses of the Quran that include commands to seek forgiveness. He raises his hands with the back of the hand towards the sky [i.e., palms downward] and supplicates using the supplication of the Prophet ﷺ that includes "*Allāhumma sqinā ghaythan mughīthan…*" ‹…

«اللَّهُمَّ اسْقِنَا غَيْثًا مغيثًا هَنِيئًا مَرِيئًا مَرِيعًا سَحًّا عامًّا غَدَقًا طَبَقًا مُجَلَّلًا دائمًا»

"Allāhumma sqinā ghaythan mughīthan hanīʾan marīʿan saḥḥan ʿāmman ghadaqan ṭabaqan mujalladan dāʾiman."

("O Allah, send us rain; wholesome, healthy, torrential, wide-spread, pouring, in sheets, drenching, continuous rain.")

«اللَّهُمَّ اسْقِنَا الغَيْثَ وَلا تَجْعَلْنَا مِنَ القَانِطِين»

"Allāhumma sqinā l-ghaytha wa lā tajʿalnā mina l-qāniṭīn."

("O Allah, give us rain and make us not of those who despair.")

«اللَّهُمَّ اجْعَلْها سُقْيا رَحْمَةٍ وَلا تَجْعَلْها سُقْيا عَذابٍ وَلا مَحقٍ وَلا بَلاءٍ، وَلا هَدْمٍ وَلا غَرَقٍ»

"Allāhumma jʿalhā suqya raḥmatin wa lā tajʿalhā suqyā ʿadhābin wa lā mahqin wa lā balāʾin wa lā hadmin wa lā gharaqin."

("O Allah, make it a water of mercy and do not make it a shower of torture, or wrath, trial, destruction or drowning.")

«اللَّهُمَ إِنَّ بِالعِبادِ وَالبِلادِ مِنَ الجَهْدِ وَالْجُوْعِ وَالضَّنْكِ ما لا نَشْكُو إلاّ إِلَيْكَ»

"Allāhumma inna bi-l-ʿibādi wa-l-bilādi mina l-jahdi wa l-jūʿi wa ḍ-ḍanki mā lā tashkū illā ilayka."

("O Allah, servants and cities are in distress, hunger and want, from which we can ask none but You for relief.")

«اللَّهُمَّ أَنْبِتْ لَنَا الزَّرْعَ وَأَدِرَّ لَنَا الضَّرْعَ وَأَنْزِلْ عَلَيْنَا مِنْ بَرَكَاتِ السَّمَاءِ وَأَنْبِتْ لَنَا مِنْ بَرَكَاتِ الأَرْضِ، وَاكْشِفْ عَنَّا مِنَ البَلاءِ مَا لاَ يَكْشِفُهُ غَيْرُكَ»

"Allāhumma anbit lana z-zarʿa wa adirra lana ḍ-ḍarʿa wa anzil ʿalaynā min barakāti s-samāʾi wa anbit lanā min barakāti l-arḍi wa kshif ʿannā mina l-balāʾi mā lā yakshifuhu ghayruka."

("O Allah, make the crops grow and the milk of the livestock flow, and send down the blessings of the sky upon us and bring forth for us the blessings of the earth. Raise from us the affliction that none but You can lift.")

«اللَّهُمَّ إِنَّا نَسْتَغْفِرُكَ إِنَّكَ كُنْتَ غَفَّارًا فَأَرْسِلِ السَّمَاءَ عَلَيْنَا مِدْرَارًا»

"Allāhumma innā nastaghfiruka innaka kunta ghaffāran fa arsili s-samā'a ʿalaynā midrāran."

("O Allah, we seek forgiveness from You since You are Oft-Forgiving, so let loose the sky upon us in torrents.")›

وَإِنْ كَثُرَ ٱلْمَطَرُ حَتَّى خِيفَ سُنَّ قَوْلُ: «اَللَّهُمَّ حَوَالَيْنَا وَلَا عَلَيْنَا، اَللَّهُمَّ عَلَى ٱلظِّرَابِ وَالْآكَامِ وَبُطُونِ ٱلْأَوْدِيَةِ وَمَنَابِتِ ٱلشَّجَرِ» ﴿رَبَّنَا وَلَا تُحَمِّلْنَا مَا لَا طَاقَةَ لَنَا بِهِ﴾ (اَلْبَقَرَة: ٢٨٦) اَلْآيَةَ.

If it rains so abundantly that there is fear, it is recommended to say, "*Allāhumma ḥawālaynā wa lā ʿalayhnā, Allāhumma ʿalā ẓ-ẓirābi wa l-akāmi wa buṭūni l-awdiyati wa manābiti sh-shajari,*" ("O Allah, around us, not upon us. O Allah, upon the hills and bluffs, upon the thickets and valley floors") "*rabbanā wa lā tuḥammilnā mā lā ṭāqata lanā bihi*" [Q2:286].

3

FUNERALS

كِتَابُ الجَنَائِزِ

Sickness and Death

تَرْكُ اَلدَّوَاءِ أَفْضَلُ وسُنَّ اِسْتِعْدَادٌ لِلْمَوْتِ، وَإِكْثَارٌ مِنْ ذِكْرِهِ، وَعِيَادَةُ مُسْلِمٍ غَيْرِ مُبْتَدِعٍ وَتَذْكِيرُهُ اَلتَّوْبَةَ وَالْوَصِيَّةَ، فَإِذَا نَزَلَ بِهِ سُنَّ تَعَاهُدُ بَلِّ حَلْقِهِ بِمَاءٍ أَوْ شَرَابٍ، وَتَنْدِيَةُ شَفَتَيْهِ، وَتَلْقِينُهُ: «لَا إِلَهَ إِلَّا اَللهُ» مَرَّةً، وَلَا يُزَادُ عَنْ ثَلَاثٍ إِلَّا أَنْ يَتَكَلَّمَ فَيُعَادَ بِرِفْقٍ، وَقِرَاءَةُ اَلْفَاتِحَةِ وَيَاسِينَ عِنْدَهُ.

وَتَوْجِيهُهُ إِلَى اَلْقِبْلَةِ، وَإِذَا مَاتَ تَغْمِيضُ عَيْنَيْهِ وَشَدُّ لَحْيَيْهِ، وَتَلْيِينُ مَفَاصِلِهِ وَخَلْعُ ثِيَابِهِ، وَسَتْرُهُ بِثَوْبٍ وَوَضْعُ حَدِيدَةٍ أَوْ نَحْوِهَا عَلَى بَطْنِهِ، وَجَعْلُهُ عَلَى سَرِيرِ غَسْلِهِ مُتَوَجِّهًا مُنْحَدِرًا نَحْوَ رِجْلَيْهِ، وَإِسْرَاعُ تَجْهِيزِهِ، وَيَجِبُ فِي نَحْوِ تَفْرِيقِ وَصِيَّتِهِ وَقَضَاءِ دَيْنِهِ.

Forgoing medical treatment is superior ‹since it is closer to realizing *tawakkul*. Treatment is not obligatory, even when one thinks it to be efficacious; since the true agent of benefit and harm is Allah Sublime and Majestic is He, and treatment in itself has no efficacy.[1] It is unlawful to treat using things that are unlawful.›

It is recommended to prepare for death; to frequently remember it; to visit sick Muslims who are not innovators, and to remind them to repent and to make a will.

---

1. Some scholars consider treatment better, obligatory in general or when one is confident of its efficacy. Al-Mardāwī, *Al-Inṣāf fī Maʿrifat al-Rājiḥ min al-Khilāf* (Beirut: Dār Iḥyā' al-Turāth al-ʿArabī, n.d.), 2:463.

When someone is on the verge of death, it is recommended to keep their throat wet with water or something to drink, to moisten their lips, to gently prompt them to say "*Lā ilāha ilā Llāh*" a single time (one does not exceed doing this three times unless they speak, and then it is repeated, gently); to recite Al-Fātiḥah [Q1] and Yā Sīn [Q36] to him; to face him towards the direction of prayer.

When he dies, ‹it is recommended› to close his eyes; to bind his jaws ‹by tying something around them to hold them together›; to manipulate his joints so they remain flexible; to remove his clothing and cover him with a long shirt; to place iron or the like ‹e.g., a mirror› on his stomach ‹to keep it from bloating›; to place him on the bed where he will be washed, facing the direction of prayer, with his body angled so his feet are lower; to rapidly prepare him.

It is obligatory to hastily execute his bequests and pay off his debts.

Washing and Shrouding the Deceased

(فَصْلٌ) وَإِذَا أَخَذَ فِي غُسْلِهِ سَتَرَ عَوْرَتَهُ، وَسُنَّ سَتْرُ كُلِّهِ عَنْ اَلْعُيُونِ، وَكُرِهَ حُضُورُ غَيْرِ مُعِينٍ ثُمَّ نَوَى وَسَمَّى، وَهُمَا كَفِي غُسْلِ حَيٍّ ثُمَّ يَرْفَعُ رَأْسَ غَيْرِ حَامِلٍ إِلَى قُرْبِ جُلُوسٍ، وَيَعْصِرُ بَطْنَهُ بِرِفْقٍ، وَيُكْثِرُ اَلْمَاءَ حِينَئِذٍ ثُمَّ يَلُفُّ عَلَى يَدِهِ خِرْقَةً فَيُنَجِّيهِ بِهَا، وَحَرُمَ مَسُّ عَوْرَةِ مَنْ لَهُ سَبْعٌ.

When ‹the washer› begins washing him, his nakedness is covered. It is recommended to cover him completely from onlookers. It is offensive for anyone to attend other than an assistant.

[The washer] makes an intention and says, "*Bismi Llāh*" just as for washing the living ‹in that they are obligatory and they are dropped out of forgetfulness and ignorance›. If the deceased is not pregnant, the washer lifts the deceased's head until he is close to seated, gently presses the stomach, and uses a great deal of water ‹to wash away whatever is expelled from the stomach and to remove its smell›. He then wraps a cloth on his hand and cleans the deceased's private parts. It is unlawful to touch the nakedness of a deceased who is seven years of age or older.

ثُمَّ يُدْخِلُ إِصْبَعَيْهِ وَعَلَيْهَا خِرْقَةٌ مَبْلُولَةٌ فِي فَمِهِ، فَيَمْسَحُ أَسْنَانَهُ، وَفِي مَنْخِرَيْهِ فَيُنَظِّفُهُمَا بِلَا إِدْخَالِ مَاءٍ، ثُمَّ يُوَضِّئُهُ وَيَغْسِلُ رَأْسَهُ وَلِحْيَتَهُ بِرَغْوَةِ ٱلسِّدْرِ وَبَدَنَهُ بِثُفْلِهِ، ثُمَّ يُفِيضُ عَلَيْهِ ٱلْمَاءَ، وَسُنَّ تَثْلِيثٌ وَتَيَامُنٌ وَإِمْرَارُ يَدِهِ كُلَّ مَرَّةٍ، وَمَاءٌ حَارٌّ وَخِلَالٌ وَأُشْنَانٌ بِلَا حَاجَةٍ، وَتَسْرِيحُ شَعْرِهِ.

The washer then inserts his fingers, wrapped in a wet cloth, into the mouth of the deceased and wipes his teeth; and into the nostrils but without introducing water. The washer then performs ablution for the deceased, washes his head and beard using lote-tree froth, and his body with the lote-tree water residue. The washer then pours the water over the deceased.

It is recommended to do ‹the washing› three times ‹as with washing someone alive, except that ablution is done during the first›, to do the right side first, and to pass the hand over the stomach each time. If the deceased is not clean ‹with three times›, more washings are added until he is.

It is offensive to limit to a single washing.

When there is no need to do so, it is offensive to use hot water, to floss the deceased's teeth, to use saltwort [*ashnān*], and to comb the deceased's hair.

وَسُنَّ كَافُورٌ وَسِدْرٌ فِي ٱلْأَخِيرَةِ، وَخِضَابُ شَعْرٍ، وَقَصُّ شَارِبٍ، وَتَقْلِيمُ أَظْفَارٍ إِنْ طَالَا، وَتَنْشِيفٌ، وَيُجَنَّبُ مُحْرِمٌ مَاتَ مَا يُجَنَّبُ فِي حَيَاتِهِ وَسِقْطٌ لِأَرْبَعَةِ أَشْهُرٍ كَمَوْلُودٍ حَيًّا، وَإِذَا تَعَذَّرَ غُسْلُ مَيِّتٍ يُمِّمَ، وَسُنَّ تَكْفِينُ رَجُلٍ فِي ثَلَاثِ لَفَائِفَ بِيضٍ بَعْدَ تَبْخِيرِهَا، وَيُجْعَلُ ٱلْحَنُوطُ فِيمَا بَيْنَهَا، وَمِنْهُ بِقُطْنٍ بَيْنَ أَلْيَيْهِ، وَالْبَاقِي عَلَى مَنَافِذِ وَجْهِهِ وَمَوَاضِعِ سُجُودِهِ، ثُمَّ يَرُدَّ طَرَفَ ٱلْعُلْيَا مِنَ ٱلْجَانِبِ ٱلْأَيْسَرِ عَلَى شِقِّهِ ٱلْأَيْمَنِ، ثُمَّ ٱلْأَيْمَنَ عَلَى ٱلْأَيْسَرِ، ثُمَّ ٱلثَّانِيَةَ وَالثَّالِثَةَ كَذَلِكَ، وَيَجْعَلُ أَكْثَرَ ٱلْفَاضِلِ عِنْدَ رَأْسِهِ.

It is recommended to use camphor and lote-tree in the final washing, to dye the hair ‹of the head for a woman, and the beard for a man›, to trim the mustache, to pare long nails, and to dry them.

A pilgrim who died is kept away from the same things that pilgrims avoid while alive.

A miscarriage that is four months or more is treated as though it was born alive.

When it is not possible to wash the deceased, dry ablution is performed ‹and he is shrouded and prayed over›.

It is recommended that a man be shrouded in three white cloths which have been steam-scented. ‹It is recommended to spread out the shrouds, one atop the other, so the deceased can be placed upon the three simultaneously.› Perfume [*ḥanūt*] should be sprinkled in between them. Some perfume [*ḥanūt*] should be applied to cotton that is then placed between the buttocks, the openings of the face ‹like his eyes, mouth, nose, and ears›, and the places that one prostrates upon ‹his forehead, hands, knees, and the tips of his toes›.

Then the edge of the uppermost shroud [touching the deceased] is passed from the left side over his right side, then the right side over the left. And likewise with the second and third shroud. The majority of the excess [length of the] shroud should be at his head.

وَسُنَّ لِامْرَأَةٍ خَمْسَةُ أَثْوَابٍ: إِزَارٌ وَخِمَارٌ وَقَمِيصٌ وَلِفَافَتَانِ، وَصَغِيرَةٍ قَمِيصٌ وَلِفَافَتَانِ، وَالْوَاجِبُ ثَوْبٌ يَسْتُرُ جَمِيعَ ٱلْمَيِّتِ.

It is recommended that women be buried in five garments: a long skirt [*izār*], a head covering [*khimār*], a shirt [*qamīṣ*], and two shrouds.

A young girl is buried in a shirt and two shrouds.

The obligation is a single garment covering the entire body.

The Funeral Prayer

(فَصْلٌ) وَتَسْقُطُ ٱلصَّلَاةُ عَلَيْهِ بِمُكَلَّفٍ، وَتُسَنُّ جَمَاعَةً، وَقِيَامُ إِمَامٍ وَمُنْفَرِدٍ عِنْدَ صَدْرِ رَجُلٍ وَوَسَطِ امْرَأَةٍ، ثُمَّ يُكَبِّرُ أَرْبَعًا، يَقْرَأُ بَعْدَ ٱلْأُولَى وَالتَّعَوُّذِ ٱلْفَاتِحَةَ بِلَا اِسْتِفْتَاحٍ، وَيُصَلِّي عَلَى ٱلنَّبِيِّ ﷺ بَعْدَ ٱلثَّانِيَةِ، وَيَدْعُو بَعْدَ ٱلثَّالِثَةِ، وَالْأَفْضَلُ بِشَيْءٍ مِمَّا

وَرَدَ، وَمِنْهُ: «اَللَّهُمَّ اغْفِرْ لِحَيِّنَا وَمَيِّتِنَا، وَشَاهِدِنَا وَغَائِبِنَا، وَصَغِيرِنَا وَكَبِيرِنَا، وَذَكَرِنَا وَأُنْثَانَا، إِنَّكَ تَعْلَمُ مُنْقَلَبَنَا وَمَثْوَانَا، وَأَنْتَ عَلَى كُلِّ شَيْءٍ قَدِيرٌ» «اَللَّهُمَّ مَنْ أَحْيَيْتَهُ مِنَّا فَأَحْيِهِ عَلَى اَلْإِسْلَامِ وَالسُّنَّةِ، وَمَنْ تَوَفَّيْتَهُ مِنَّا فَتَوَفَّهُ عَلَيْهِمَا، اَللَّهُمَّ اغْفِرْ لَهُ وَارْحَمْهُ وَعَافِهِ وَاعْفُ عَنْهُ، وَأَكْرِمْ نُزُلَهُ، وَأَوْسِعْ مُدْخَلَهُ، وَاغْسِلْهُ بِالْمَاءِ وَالثَّلْجِ وَالْبَرَدِ وَنَقِّهِ مِنَ اَلذُّنُوبِ وَالْخَطَايَا كَمَا يُنَقَّى اَلثَّوْبُ اَلْأَبْيَضُ مِنَ اَلدَّنَسِ، وَأَبْدِلْهُ دَارًا خَيْرًا مِنْ دَارِهِ، وَزَوْجًا خَيْرًا مِنْ زَوْجِهِ، وَأَدْخِلْهُ اَلْجَنَّةَ، وَأَعِذْهُ مِنْ عَذَابِ اَلْقَبْرِ، وَعَذَابِ اَلنَّارِ، وَافْسَحْ لَهُ فِي قَبْرِهِ وَنَوِّرْ لَهُ فِيهِ».

The obligation for the Funeral Prayer lifts when performed by a responsible individual ‹even a female or hermaphrodite›.

Its performance is recommended in congregation; and for the imam and an individual praying separately to stand at the chest of a male deceased, and at the middle of a female deceased.

‹While standing and after the intention›, four sayings of "*Allāhu akbar*" are made. After the first, one seeks protection [saying "*aʿūdhu bi-Llāhi mina sh-shayṭāni r-rajīm*"] ‹and says "*Bismi Llāhi r-raḥmāni r-rāḥīm*"›, and reads Al-Fātiḥah (but without reading the opening supplication). After the second, one supplicates upon the Prophet ﷺ. After the third, one supplicates for the deceased. It is best to use something transmitted [from the Prophet ﷺ]. These include:

> "*Allāhumma ghfir li-ḥayyinā wa mayyitinā wa shāhidinā wa ghāʾibina wa ṣaghīrinā wa kabīrinā wa dhukurinā wa unthānā innaka taʿlamu munqalibanā wa mathwānā wa anta ʿalā kulli shayʾin qadīr*"
>
> ("O Allah, forgive those of us who are living and those of us who are dead, those of us who are present and those of us who are absent, our young and our old, our male and our female. O Allah, you know our final destiny and abode, and You are capable of all things.")
>
> "*Allāhumma man aḥyatahu minnā fa-ḥyihi ʿalā l-islāmi*

wa s-sunnati wa man tawwafaytahi minnā fa-tawaffahu ʿalāyhimā, Allāhumma ghfir lahu wa-rḥamhu wa-ʿfihu ʿanhu wa-krim nuzulahu wa awsiʿ mudkhalahu wa-ghsilhu bi l-māʾi wa th-thalji wa l-baradi wa naqqihi mina dh-dhunūbi wa l-khaṭāyā kamā yunaqqā th-thaubu al-abyaḍu mina d-danas wa-bdilhu dāran khayran min dārihi wa zawjan khayran min zawjihi wa-dkhilhu l-jannat wa-aʿidhhu min ʿadhābi l-qabri wa ʿadhābi n-nār wa-fsaḥ lahu fī qabrihi wa nawwir lahu fīhi"

("O Allah, to whomsoever of us Thou givest life grant him life [as a follower of] Islam and the Sunnah, and whomsoever of us Thou takest in death take him in death as a follower of them both. O Allah, forgive him and grant him mercy. Grant him ease and respite. Make his resting place a noble one, and facilitate his entry. Wash him with water, snow and hail. Purify him from sins and mistakes just as a white garment is cleansed of dirt. Exchange for him a better home than his home [than he had in this life] and a spouse better than his spouse. Grant him entrance to Paradise and protect him from the trials of the grave and the torture of Hell Fire. Make his grave spacious and grant him light while in it").

وَإِنْ كَانَ صَغِيرًا أَوْ مَجْنُونًا قَالَ: «اَللَّهُمَّ اِجْعَلْهُ ذُخْرًا لِوَالِدَيْهِ وَفَرَطًا وَأَجْرًا وَشَفِيعًا مُجَابًا، اَللَّهُمَّ ثَقِّلْ بِهِ مَوَازِينَهُمَا، وَأَعْظِمْ بِهِ أُجُورَهُمَا، وَأَلْحِقْهُ بِصَالِحِ سَلَفِ اَلْمُؤْمِنِينَ، وَاجْعَلْهُ فِي كَفَالَةِ إِبْرَاهِيمَ، وَقِهِ بِرَحْمَتِكَ عَذَابَ اَلْجَحِيمِ» وَيَقِفُ بَعْدَ اَلرَّابِعَةِ قَلِيلًا، وَيُسَلِّمُ وَيَرْفَعُ يَدَيْهِ مَعَ كُلِّ تَكْبِيرَةٍ.

If the deceased is a minor or insane, one says:

"*Allāhumma jʿalhu dhukhran li wālidayhi wa faraṭan wa ajran wa shafīʿan mujāban, Allāhumma thaqqil bihi mawāzīnahum wa-ʿaẓam bihi ujūrahum wa-lḥiqhu bi-ṣāliḥ salafi l-mu'minīn wa-jʿalhu fī kafālati Ibrāhīma wa-qihi bi-raḥmatika ʿadhāba l-jaḥīm"*

("O Allah, make him a bounty for his parents, a herald to happiness, and a intercessor who[se supplication] is answered. O Allah, make him a heavy weight on their scales [of good deeds], and magnify their rewards because of him. Place him with the righteous believers who went before. Entrust him to Ibrāhīm [peace be upon him]. Protect him with Your mercy from the torture of Hell").

After the fourth ‹*takbīr*›, one stands for a short while and says "*As-salāmu ʿalaykum.*"

The hands are raised with each saying of "*Allāhu akbar.*"

Carrying and Burying the Deceased

وَسُنَّ تَرْبِيعٌ فِي حَمْلِهَا، وَإِسْرَاعٌ وَكَوْنُ مَاشٍ أَمَامَهَا، وَرَاكِبٍ لِحَاجَةٍ خَلْفَهَا، وَقُرْبٌ مِنْهَا، وَكَوْنُ قَبْرٍ لَحْدًا، وَقَوْلُ مُدْخِلٍ: «بِسْمِ اَللهِ، وَعَلَى مِلَّةِ رَسُولِ اَللهِ ﷺ وَلَحْدُهُ عَلَى شِقِّهِ اَلْأَيْمَنِ، وَيَجِبُ اسْتِقْبَالُهُ اَلْقِبْلَةَ، وَكُرِهَ -بِلَا حَاجَةٍ- جُلُوسٌ تَابِعِهَا قَبْلَ وَضْعِهَا، وَتَجْصِيصُ قَبْرٍ، وَبِنَاءٌ وَكِتَابَةٌ، وَمَشْيٌ، وَجُلُوسٌ عَلَيْهِ، وَإِدْخَالُهُ شَيْئًا مَسَّتْهُ اَلنَّارُ، وَتَبَسُّمٌ، وَحَدِيثٌ بِأَمْرِ اَلدُّنْيَا عِنْدَهُ. وَحَرُمَ دَفْنُ اِثْنَيْنِ فَأَكْثَرَ فِي قَبْرٍ إِلَّا لِضَرُورَةٍ، وَأَيُّ قُرْبَةٍ فُعِلَتْ وَجُعِلَ ثَوَابُهَا لِمُسْلِمٍ حَيٍّ أَوْ مَيِّتٍ نَفَعَهُ.

It is recommended for four to carry it ‹the deceased, putting the poles [of the container or pallet used while transporting the deceased] on their shoulders›, to do so quickly, to walk ahead of it and for those in need to ride behind, and to be close to it.

‹It is recommended› for the grave to be a niche ‹carved out at the bottom of the grave, towards the direction of prayer, *laḥd*›; for the person placing the body to say, "*Bismi Llāhi ʿalā millati rasūli Llāh*" ("In the name of Allah, and upon the religion of the Messenger of

Allah"); and to place it in the niche on its right side – with it being obligatory to face it towards the direction of prayer.

It is offensive for those accompanying the procession to sit needlessly before the deceased has been placed; to plaster, ‹bury within a casket,› build ‹a dome or something else› over, or write on a grave; to walk over or sit on it; to place anything in the grave touched by fire ‹or made of iron›; and to smile or speak about worldly affairs in proximity of the deceased.

It is unlawful to bury two [bodies] in a single grave without necessity ‹or need› to do so ‹e.g., a large number of bodies due to killing or the like, or the lack of people to bury them›.

Any pious act [*qurbah*] performed ‹by a Muslim› with its reward ‹or part of it› made ‹i.e., donated› to a living or a deceased Muslim will be beneficial ‹through obtaining the reward, even to the Messenger of Allah ﷺ›.

وَسُنَّ لِرِجَالٍ زِيَارَةُ قَبْرِ مُسْلِمٍ، وَالْقِرَاءَةِ عِنْدَهُ، وَمَا يُخَفِّفُ عَنْهُ، وَلَوْ بِجَعْلِ جَرِيدَةٍ رَطْبَةٍ فِي اَلْقَبْرِ، وَقَوْلُ زَائِرٍ وَمَارٍّ بِهِ: «اَلسَّلَامُ عَلَيْكُمْ دَارَ قَوْمٍ مُؤْمِنِينَ، وَإِنَّا إِنْ شَاءَ اَللهُ بِكُمْ لَاحِقُونَ، يَرْحَمُ اَللهُ اَلْمُسْتَقْدِمِينَ مِنْكُمْ وَالْمُسْتَأْخِرِينَ، نَسْأَلُ اَللهَ لَنَا وَلَكُمْ اَلْعَافِيَةَ، اَللَّهُمَّ لَا تَحْرِمْنَا أَجْرَهُمْ، وَلَا تَفْتِنَّا بَعْدَهُمْ، وَاغْفِرْ لَنَا وَلَهُمْ».

It is recommended for men to visit a Muslim's grave ‹without traveling›.

‹It is offensive for women to visit graves. If she knows she will do something that is unlawful, it is unlawful for her to go out for a visit – except to the grave of the Prophet ﷺ and the grave of his two Companions (may Allah be pleased with them), as visiting them is recommended for men and women. If a woman happens to pass by a grave in her path, it is good if she greets and prays for its occupant.›

‹It is recommended› to recite Quran to him, and to do whatever will ease his affairs – even placing a palm frond ‹or the like› on the grave.

‹It is recommended› that a visitor or someone passing by say

"*As-salāmu ʿalaykum dāra qaumin mu'minīn wa innā in shā Allāhu bikum lāḥiqūn, yarḥamu Llāhu l-mustaqdimīn minkum wa l-muta'akhirīn, nas'alu Llāha lana wa lakuma l-ʿāfiyata, Allāhumma lā taḥrimnā ajrahum wa lā taftinnā baʿdahum wa-ghfir lanā wa lahum*"

("Peace be upon you, inhabitants of the dwellings who are of the community of the believers. If Allah wills we shall join you. May Allah grant mercy to those of you who hasten forward and those of you who lag behind. We ask Allah for ourselves and for you for a respite. O Allah, do not deprive us of his reward, nor afflict us after him. [O Allah,] grant us and him forgiveness").

وَتَعْزِيَةُ ٱلْمُصَابِ بِالْمَيِّتِ سُنَّةٌ، وَيَجُوزُ ٱلْبُكَاءُ عَلَيْهِ، وَحَرُمَ نَدْبٌ، وَنِيَاحَةٌ، وَشَقُّ ثَوْبٍ، وَلَطْمُ خَدٍّ وَنَحْوُهُ.

It is recommended to console ‹Muslims› touched by a death ‹before burial and after, even when the deceased is a child or a friend or a neighbor. One does not omit it if the person rips his clothing as something rightful is not abandoned due to the presence of folly. The consoler says, "*aʿẓam Allāhu ajraka wa aḥsana ʿazā'aka wa ghafara li mayyitik*" ("May Allah greaten your reward, perfect your consolation, and forgive your deceased"). The response is, "*istajāba Allāhu duʿā'aka wa raḥimanā wa iyyāka*" ("May Allah answer your supplication, and grant us both mercy"). If the consoler forbids him [from ripping his clothing], it is good›.

It is permissible to cry for the deceased. ‹It is recommended for someone touched by a death to say, "*innā li-Llāhi wa innā ilayhi rājiʿūn, Allāhumma jburnī fī muṣībatī wa khluf lī khayran minhā*" ("Verily we belong to Allah and unto Him will we return. O Allah, improve me during my difficulty and give me something better than it")[2] and to then pray two prayer-cycles and be patient.› It is unlawful to weepingly eulogize, to wail, to tear one's clothing, to strike one's cheeks, and the like ‹e.g., to scream, or to pull out or shave one's hair›.

‹The dead know of their visitors on Friday before the sun rises. [Shaykh ʿAbd al-Qādir al-Jaylānī] says in *Al-Ghunyā* that they always know of their visitors, but this time is more emphatic. The dead are hurt by objectionable acts in their presence, and they benefit by good deeds. It is obligatory to believe that the dead are tortured in their graves.›

2. The commentary *Kashf al-Mukhaddarāt* has "*Allāhuma jburnī*" ("O Allah improve me..." or "O Allah aid me..."). This phrasing" in found in a similar narration transmitted in Abū Naʿīm's *Al-Musnad al-Mustakhrāj ʿalā Ṣaḥīḥ Muslim*, 3:7 #2056. However, other books use the well-known phrasing "*Allāhumma jirnī*" ("O Allah, reward me for...").

4

ZAKAT

كِتَابُ الزَّكَاةِ

تَجِبُ فِي خَمْسَةِ أَشْيَاءَ: بَهِيمَةِ ٱلْأَنْعَامِ وَنَقْدٍ وَعَرْضِ تِجَارَةٍ، وَخَارِجٍ مِنْ ٱلْأَرْضِ، وَثِمَارٍ، بِشَرْطِ إِسْلَامٍ، وَحُرِّيَّةٍ، وَمِلْكِ نِصَابٍ، وَاسْتِقْرَارِهِ وَسَلَامَةٍ مِنْ دَيْنٍ يُنْقِصُ ٱلنِّصَابَ، وَمُضِيِّ حَوْلٍ إِلَّا فِي مُعَشَّرٍ وَنِتَاجِ سَائِمَةٍ، وَرِبْحِ تِجَارَةٍ وَإِنْ نَقَصَ فِي [بَعْضِ] ٱلْحَوْلِ بِبَيْعٍ أَوْ غَيْرِهِ لَا فِرَارًا

وَإِذَا قَبَضَ ٱلدَّيْنَ زَكَّاهُ لِمَا مَضَى وَشُرِطَ لَهَا فِي بَهِيمَةِ ٱلْأَنْعَامِ سَوْمٌ أَيْضًا.

It ‹alms [*zakāh*]› is obligatory from five things:
‹1› livestock ‹camels, cows, sheep [and goats]›;
‹2› ‹gold and silver› currency;
‹3› trade goods;
‹4› anything extracted from the earth; and,
‹5› fruit.

[Its] conditions are: being Muslim; free; owning the minimum amount [*nisāb*]; ‹its ownership being› established [*istiqrārihi*] ‹by being placed where, for example, dates are collected and dried›; being free of debts reducing it below the minimum amount; the passing of a lunar year – except in things from which tenths are owed ‹e.g., honey, treasures, ore›, offspring of grazed [livestock], and profit from trade.

The duration is interrupted if the minimum amount falls short during part of the year via a ‹valid› sale or something else ‹like exchanging a minimum amount of something from which alms are owed for something of another category, like cows or camels for something else› – but without intending to avoid paying zakat. But it is not interrupted if an item is exchanged for another of the same category [*jinsihi*] ‹like a sheep for a sheep›.

If one takes possession of a debt, one pays alms for what has passed.

Another condition for livestock is grazing.

وَأَقَلُّ نِصَابِ إِبِلٍ: خَمْسٌ، وَفِيهَا شَاةٌ، وَفِي عَشْرٍ شَاتَانِ، وَفِي خَمْسَ عَشْرَةَ ثَلَاثٌ، وَفِي عِشْرِينَ أَرْبَعٌ، وَفِي خَمْسٍ وَعِشْرِينَ: بِنْتُ مَخَاضٍ، وَهِيَ الَّتِي لَهَا سَنَةٌ، وَفِي سِتَّةٍ وَثَلَاثِينَ بِنْتُ لَبُونٍ، وَهِيَ الَّتِي لَهَا سَنَتَانِ، وَفِي سِتٍّ وَأَرْبَعِينَ حِقَّةٌ، وَهِيَ الَّتِي لَهَا ثَلَاثٌ، وَفِي إِحْدَى وَسِتِّينَ جَذَعَةٌ وَهِيَ الَّتِي لَهَا أَرْبَعٌ، وَفِي سِتٍّ وَسَبْعِينَ بِنْتَا لَبُونٍ، وَفِي إِحْدَى وَسِتِّينَ حِقَّتَانِ، وَفِي مِائَةٍ وَإِحْدَى وَعِشْرِينَ ثَلَاثُ بَنَاتِ لَبُونٍ، ثُمَّ فِي كُلِّ أَرْبَعِينَ بِنْتُ لَبُونٍ، وَفِي كُلِّ خَمْسِينَ حِقَّةٌ.

The minimum amount [*niṣāb*]:

for camels is five, from which one *shāh*[1] is owed;
for ten ‹camels›, two *shāhs* [are owed];
for fifteen ‹camels›: three [*shāh*s];
for twenty: four;
for twenty-five: one *bint makhāḍ* (a one-year-old female camel);
for thirty-six: one *bint labūn* (a two-year old female camel);
for forty-six: one *ḥiqqah* (a three-year-old female camel);
from sixty-one: one *jadhʿah* (a four-year-old female camel);
from seventy-six: two *bint labūn*s;
from ninety-one: two *ḥiqqah*s; and,
from one-hundred and twenty-one: three *bint labūn*s.

Then:

from every forty: one *bint labūn*; and,
from every fifty: one *ḥiqqah*.

1. The author clarifies what is intended by *shāḥ* in the schedule for sheep and goats. He explains that a "*shāḥ* is a one-year old female goat, or half ‹a year› for a lamb."

وَأَقَلُّ نِصَابِ ٱلْبَقَرِ: ثَلَاثُونَ، وَفِيهَا تَبِيعٌ، وَهُوَ ٱلَّذِي لَهُ سَنَةٌ، أَوْ تَبِيعَةٌ، وَفِي أَرْبَعِينَ مُسِنَّةٌ، وَهِيَ ٱلَّتِي لَهَا سَنَتَانِ، وَفِي سِتِّينَ تَبِيعَانِ، ثُمَّ فِي كُلِّ ثَلَاثِينَ تَبِيعٌ، وَفِي كُلِّ أَرْبَعِينَ مُسِنَّةٌ.

The minimum amount [*niṣāb*]:

for cows is thirty, from which one male or female *tabīʿ* is owed ([a *tabīʿ*] is a one-year-old calf;

for forty ‹cows›, one *musinnah* is owed ([a *musinnah*] is a two-year-old female cow); and,
for sixty, two *tabīʿ*s are owed.

Then:

for every thirty ‹cows›, a *tabīʿ* [is owed]; and,
for every forty, a *musinnah* [is owed].

وَأَقَلُّ نِصَابِ ٱلْغَنَمِ: أَرْبَعُونَ، وَفِيهَا شَاةٌ، وَفِي مِائَةٍ وَإِحْدَى وَعِشْرِينَ شَاتَانِ، وَفِي مِائَتَيْنِ وَوَاحِدَةٍ ثَلَاثٌ [إِلَى أَرْبَعِمِائَةٍ] ثُمَّ فِي كُلِّ مِائَةٍ شَاةٌ، وَالشَّاةُ بِنْتُ سَنَةٍ مِنَ ٱلْمَعْزِ، وَنِصْفُهَا مِنَ ٱلضَّأْنِ، وَٱلْخِلْطَةُ فِي بَهِيمَةِ ٱلْأَنْعَامِ بِشَرْطِهَا تُصَيِّرُ ٱلْمَالَيْنِ كَالْوَاحِدِ.

The minimum amount [*niṣāb*]:

for sheep and goats is forty, from which one *shāh* is owed;
for one-hundred and twenty-one, two *shāh*s are owed; and,
for two-hundred and one: three.

[Three are owed] up until four-hundred; and, after that, in every hundred is one *shāh*.

A *shāh* is a one-year old female goat, or half ‹a year› for a lamb.

Mixing livestock according to its conditions renders two properties like one.

Agriculture

(فَصْلٌ) وَتَجِبُ فِي كُلِّ مَكِيلٍ مُدَّخَرٍ خَرَجَ مِنْ اَلْأَرْضِ، وَنِصَابُهُ خَمْسَةُ أَوْسُقٍ، وَهِيَ ثَلَاثُمِائَةٍ وَاثْنَانِ وَأَرْبَعُونَ رِطْلًا وَسِتَّةُ أَسْبَاعِ رِطْلٍ بِالدِّمَشْقِيِّ وَشُرِطَ مِلْكُهُ وَقْتَ وُجُوبٍ، وَهُوَ اِشْتِدَادُ حَبٍّ، وَبُدُوُّ صَلَاحِ ثَمَرٍ، وَلَا يَسْتَقِرُّ إِلَّا بِجَعْلِهَا فِي بَيْدَرٍ وَنَحْوِهِ.

Alms are obligatory from everything measured by volume and stored that comes from the earth. Its minimal amount is five *awsuqs* [1 *wasaq* = 60 *ṣāʿ*; 1 *ṣāʿ* = 2.062 kilogram; 618.6 kilogram or 1,363.8 pounds]. [Five *awsuqs*] are three-hundred and forty-two *riṭls* and six-sevenths of a *riṭl* – according to Damascene [measures]. A condition is that one own it at the time it becomes due, which is when grain becomes firm, and fruit appears to be sound. Ownership is not established unless it is placed on a threshing floor [*baydar*] or the like ‹places where grain is placed to finish ripening and dry›.

وَالْوَاجِبُ عُشْرُ مَا سُقِيَ بِلَا مَئُونَةٍ وَنِصْفُهُ فِيمَا سُقِيَ بِهَا وَثَلَاثَةُ أَرْبَاعِهِ فِيمَا سُقِيَ بِهِمَا فَإِنْ تَفَاوَتَا اُعْتُبِرَ اَلْأَكْثَرُ، وَمَعَ اَلْجَهْلِ اَلْعُشْرُ.

The obligatory amount is one-tenth for whatever is irrigated without effort, and half of this ‹one-tenth [i.e., one-twentieth]› for whatever is irrigated with effort.

Three-quarters of it ‹one-tenth [i.e., ¾ of $1/10$ = 0.075]› is obligatory for whatever is irrigated with them both ‹irrigating with and without effort›. If they are unequal, whichever is greatest is used. When it is not known, one-tenth is used.

وَفِي اَلْعَسَلِ اَلْعُشْرُ سَوَاءٌ أَخَذَهُ مِنْ مَوَاتٍ أَوْ مُلْكِهِ إِذَا بَلَغَ مِائَةً وَسِتِّينَ رِطْلًا عِرَاقِيَّةً.

From honey, one-tenth is owed (whether it is taken from abandoned lands or one's own property) when it reaches one-hundred and sixty Irāqī *riṭl*.

وَمَنْ اِسْتَخْرَجَ مِنْ مَعْدِنٍ نِصَابًا فَفِيهِ رُبُعُ ٱلْعُشْرِ فِي ٱلْحَالِ، وَفِي ٱلرِّكَازِ ٱلْخُمُسُ مُطْلَقًا، وَهُوَ مَا وُجِدَ مِنْ دَفْنِ ٱلْجَاهِلِيَّةِ.

Whoever extracts a minimum amount of ore ‹meaning anything from the earth other than earth itself, such as gold, silver, or ore the value of which reaches the minimum amount for either one – after being purified – including metals, gems, and minerals› owes one-quarter of a tenth [i.e., ¼ of $1/10$ = 0.025] immediately. One-fifth is owed from treasure, categorically [*muṭlaqan*] ‹small or large; gold, silver, or a commodity; found by a Muslim or non-Muslim; adult or minor; free or buying his freedom; rational or insane›. [Treasure] is anything found that is pre-Islamic and buried.

Gold and Silver

(فَصْلٌ) وَأَقَلُّ نِصَابِ ذَهَبٍ عِشْرُونَ مِثْقَالًا وَفِضَّةٍ مِائَتَا دِرْهَمٍ، وَيُضَمَّانِ فِي تَكْمِيلِ ٱلنِّصَابِ، وَٱلْعُرُوضُ إِلَى كُلٍّ مِنْهَا، وَٱلْوَاجِبُ فِيهِمَا رُبُعُ ٱلْعُشْرِ.

The minimum amount for gold is twenty *mithqāl*s [20 × 4.25 grams = 85 grams], and for silver two-hundred *dirhams* [200 × 2.975 grams = 595 grams]. They ‹gold and silver› are combined together to complete the minimum amount ‹so someone who owns ten *mithqāl*s of gold and one-hundred *dirham*s of silver pays alms on them both› – and for trade goods to each of them ‹so someone who owns ten *mithqāl*s of gold and trade goods worth ten *mithqāl*s, or one-hundred *dirham*s and goods worth another one-hundred *dirhams*›. The obligation for them both ‹i.e., gold and silver› is one-quarter of a tenth [i.e., ¼ × $1/10$ = 0.025].

Using Gold and Silver

وَأُبِيحَ لِرَجُلٍ مِنَ ٱلْفِضَّةِ خَاتَمٌ وَقَبِيعَةُ سَيْفٍ، وَحِلْيَةُ مِنْطَقَةٍ وَنَحْوِهِ، وَمِنَ ٱلذَّهَبِ قَبِيعَةُ سَيْفٍ وَمَا دَعَتْ إِلَيْهِ ضَرُورَةٌ كَأَنْفٍ وَلِنِسَاءٍ مِنْهُمَا مَا جَرَتْ عَادَتُهُنَّ بِلُبْسِهِ، وَلَا زَكَاةَ فِي حُلِيٍّ مُبَاحٍ أُعِدَّ لِاسْتِعْمَالٍ أَوْ عَارِيَةٍ.

Men are permitted to use silver for a ring, the pommel of a sword, or to decorate a leather waist belt and the like ‹e.g., like *khuff* and scabbards›. They are permitted to use gold for the pommel of their sword, and whatever need calls for – like a [prosthetic] nose.

Women are permitted to use gold and silver for whatever is customary for them to wear.

Alms are not required on permitted jewelry that is ready to be used or lent out.

Trade Goods

وَيَجِبُ تَقْوِيمُ عَرْضِ اَلتِّجَارَةِ بِالْأَحَظِّ لِلْفُقَرَاءِ مِنْهُمَا، وَتَخْرُجُ مِنْ قِيمَتِهِ، وَإِنْ اشْتَرَى عَرْضًا بِنِصَابٍ غَيْرَ سَائِمَةٍ بَنَى عَلَى حَوْلِهِ.

Trade goods must be assessed according to whichever is best for the poor. Zakat is extracted from its value [not its items]. If one bought trade goods with a minimum amount that is not grazing [animals], one builds upon its ‹original› duration. ‹But if one bought trade goods with a minimum zakatable amount of grazing animals for trade in exchange for a minimum zakatable amount of grazing animals that were for keeping, one builds upon their duration. If one bought trade goods in exchange for a minimal amount of grazing animals or sold them with a minimal amount of them, one does not build upon its duration due to differences between their minimal zakatable amounts and what is obligatory.›

Al-Fiṭrah Alms

(فَصْلٌ) وَتَجِبُ اَلْفِطْرَةُ عَلَى كُلِّ مُسْلِمٍ إِذَا كَانَتْ فَاضِلَةً عَنْ نَفَقَةٍ وَاجِبَةٍ يَوْمَ اَلْعِيدِ وَلَيْلَتَهُ وَحَوَائِجَ أَصْلِيَّةٍ، فَيُخْرِجُ عَنْ نَفْسِهِ وَمُسْلِمٍ يَمُونُهُ، وَتُسَنُّ عَنْ جَنِينٍ.

The *Zakāt al-Fiṭrah* alms are obligatory for every Muslim when it ‹the amount of [this] zakat› is in excess of necessary expenses for the day and night of Eid and basic needs. One pays it for himself and any Muslim he supports. It is recommended to pay it for unborn children.

وَتَجِبُ بِغُرُوبِ اَلشَّمْسِ لَيْلَةَ اَلْفِطْرِ، وَتَجُوزُ قَبْلَهُ بِيَوْمَيْنِ فَقَطْ، وَيَوْمَهُ قَبْلَ اَلصَّلَاةِ أَفْضَلُ، وَتُكْرَهُ فِي بَاقِيهِ، وَيَحْرُمُ تَأْخِيرُهَا عَنْهُ، وَتُقْضَى وُجُوبًا، وَهِيَ صَاعٌ مِنْ بُرٍّ أَوْ شَعِيرٍ أَوْ سَوِيقِهِمَا أَوْ دَقِيقِهِمَا، أَوْ تَمْرٍ، أَوْ زَبِيبٍ، أَوْ أَقِطٍ، وَالْأَفْضَلُ تَمْرٌ فَزَبِيبٌ فَبُرٌّ فَأَنْفَعُ، فَإِنْ عَدِمَتْ أَجْزَأَ كُلُّ حَبٍّ يُقْتَاتُ وَيَجُوزُ إِعْطَاءُ جَمَاعَةٍ مَا يَلْزَمُ اَلْوَاحِدَ وَعَكْسُهُ.

It becomes obligatory at sunset the night of Eid al-Fiṭr. It is permissible to pay it a maximum of two days in advance. Paying it the day of Eid al-Fiṭr before the prayer is better, and [paying it] the rest of the day is offensive. It is unlawful to delay paying it beyond the day of Eid. It is obligatory to make it up.

It[s amount] is one ṣāʿ [2.062 kilograms or 4.55 pounds] of wheat or barley, their porridge or flour; dried dates or raisins; or cottage cheese. Dates are best; then raisins, wheat, and then whatever is most beneficial. In their absence, any stored grain suffices. It is permissible to give a group what is required of an individual, and the opposite.

Alms Payment

(فَصْلٌ) وَيَجِبُ إِخْرَاجُ زَكَاةٍ عَلَى اَلْفَوْرِ مَعَ إِمْكَانِهِ، وَيُخْرِجُ وَلِيُّ صَغِيرٍ وَمَجْنُونٍ عَنْهُمَا، وَشُرِطَ لَهُ نِيَّةٌ.

It is obligatory to pay alms immediately whenever possible. The guardian of a minor or someone insane pays it for them. The intention ‹from a responsible individual› is a condition ‹when giving it›.

وَحَرُمَ نَقْلُهَا إِلَى مَسَافَةِ قَصْرٍ، إِنْ وُجِدَ أَهْلُهَا، فَإِنْ كَانَ فِي بَلَدٍ وَمَالُهُ فِي آخَرَ أَخْرَجَ زَكَاةَ اَلْمَالِ فِي بَلَدِ اَلْمَالِ، وَفِطْرَتَهُ وَفِطْرَةَ لَزِمَتْهُ فِي بَلَدِ نَفْسِهِ، وَيَجُوزُ تَعْجِيلُهَا لِحَوْلَيْنِ فَقَطْ.

It is unlawful to transport alms ‹whether it is for a relative, intense need, a breach in the defenses, or something else› beyond the distance for shortening prayers if eligible recipients exist ‹within the land where the zakatable wealth is located. If he does it anyway, it suffices›. If he is in one land and his wealth in another, alms are extracted in the land where the wealth is located. His *Zakāt al-Fiṭrah* alms for himself and whomever he must cover are extracted in his own land.

It is permissible to pay zakat a maximum of two years in advance.

وَلَا تُدْفَعُ إِلَّا إِلَى اَلْأَصْنَافِ اَلثَّمَانِيَةِ وَهُمْ: الْفُقَرَاءُ وَالْمَسَاكِيْنَ وَالعَامِلُون عَلَيْهَا وَالْمُؤْلَفَةُ قُلُوْبُهُمْ وَفِي الرِّقَابِ وَالغَارِمُوْنَ وَفِي سَبِيلِ اللهِ وَابْنُ السَّبِيْلِ.

وَيَجُوْزُ الِاقْتِصَارُ عَلَىْ وَاحِدٍ مِنْ صِنْفٍ وَالأَفْضَلُ تَعْمِيْمُهُمْ وَالتَّسْوِيَةُ بَيْنَهُمْ.

Alms are not given except to the eight categories ‹Allah Most High mentioned in the Quran [Q9:60]. It is not permissible to divert them to something else, like building mosques, bridges, burying the dead, patching holes in levees, making an endowment of Qurans, or the like. They are›:

‹1› the needy;
‹2› the poor;
‹3› alms workers;
‹4› leaders whose hearts are being softened;
‹5› slaves;
‹6› debtors;
‹7› those fighting in the path of Allah; and,
‹8› wayfarers.

It is permissible to limit oneself to a single category, but it is best to cover them all and to do so equally.

وَتُسَنُّ إِلَىْ مَنْ لَا تَلْزَمُهُ مُؤْنَتُهُ مَنْ أَقَارِبِهِ وَلَا تَدْفَعُ لِبَنِي هَاشِمٍ وَمَوَالِيْهِم، وَلَا لِأَصْلٍ وَفَرْعٍ وَعَبْدٍ وَكَافِرٍ فَإِنْ دَفَعَهَا لِمَنْ ظَنَّهُ أَهْلًا فَلَمْ يَكُنْ أَوْ بِالْعَكْسِ لَمْ تُجْزِئْهُ إِلَّا لِغَنِيٍّ ظَنَّهُ فَقِيْرًا.

It is recommended ‹to give one's alms› to one's relatives whom one is not required to support. It is not given to Banī Hāshim and their freed slaves [*mawālīhim*]; an ancestor or descendent; a slave; or a non-Muslim ‹except a leader whose heart is being softened›.

If it is given to someone who was thought eligible but was not, or the opposite; then it does not suffice – unless given to someone affluent who was thought to be needy.

Voluntary Charity

وَصَدَقَةُ التَّطَوُّعِ بِالفَاضِلِ عَنْ كِفَايَتِهِ وَكِفَايَةِ مَنْ يَمُوْنُهُ سُنَّةٌ مُؤَكَّدَةٌ وَفِيْ رَمَضَانَ وَزَمَنٍ وَمَكَانٍ فَاضِلٍ وَوَقْتِ وَحَاجَةٍ أَفْضَلُ.

Voluntary charity of whatever exceeds what suffices one and one's dependents is an emphasized recommendation. It is superior during Ramadan, in meritorious times and places, and during times of need.

5

FASTING

كِتَابُ الصِّيَامِ

يَلْزَمُ كُلَّ مُسْلِمٍ مُكَلَّفٍ قَادِرٍ بِرُؤْيَةِ الْهِلَالِ وَلَوْ مِنْ عَدْلٍ، أَوْ بِإِكْمَالِ شَعْبَانَ، أَوْ وُجُودِ مَانِعٍ مِنْ رُؤْيَتِهِ لَيْلَةَ الثَّلَاثِينَ مِنْهُ كَغَيْمٍ وَجَبَلٍ وَغَيْرِهِمَا، وَإِنْ رُئِيَ نَهَارًا فَهُوَ لِلْمُقْبِلَةِ.

وَإِنْ صَارَ أَهْلًا لِوُجُوبِهِ فِي أَثْنَائِهِ أَوْ قَدِمَ مُسَافِرٌ مُفْطِرًا، أَوْ طَهُرَتْ حَائِضٌ أَمْسَكُوا وَقَضَوْا. وَمَنْ أَفْطَرَ لِكِبَرٍ أَوْ مَرَضٍ لَا يُرْجَى بُرْؤُهُ أَطْعَمَ لِكُلِّ يَوْمٍ مِسْكِينًا.

Fasting Ramadan is required of every Muslim who is responsible and able upon sighting the crescent moon [of Ramadan] – even if sighted by a single upright male, completing thirty days of Shaʿbān, or the existence of something preventing its sighting on the night of the thirtieth of Shaʿbān (like clouds, mountains, or the like ‹e.g., smoke›). If seen during the day, it belongs to the next night.

If one becomes liable for performing its obligation during it ‹i.e., during the day, such as a minor reaches maturity while not fasting, someone sick recovers from an illness, someone insane recovers their sanity,› a traveler arrives while not fasting, or a woman's menstruation ends: one restrains [from food] and makes it up.

Whoever breaks a fast due to old age or a chronic illness feeds one poor person each day.

وَسُنَّ الْفِطْرُ لِمَرِيْضٍ يَشُقُّ عَلَيْهِ وَمُسَافِرٍ يقصُرُ وَإِنْ أَفْطَرَتْ حَامِلٌ أَوْ مُرْضِعٌ خَوْفًا عَلَىٰ أَنْفُسِهِمَا قَضَتَا فَقَطْ، أَوْ عَلَىٰ وَلَدَيْهِمَا مَعَ ٱلْإِطْعَامِ مِمَّنْ يَمُونُ ٱلْوَلَدَ وَمَنْ أُغْمِيَ عَلَيْهِ، أَوْ جُنَّ جَمِيعَ ٱلنَّهَارِ لَمْ يَصِحَّ صَوْمُهُ، وَيَقْضِي ٱلْمُغْمَى عَلَيْهِ.

Breaking the fast is recommended for someone who is sick if fasting is difficult for them, and for a traveler shortening ‹prayers›.

If a woman who is pregnant breaks her fast, or a woman who is nursing ‹breaks her fast› out of fearing for herself, she makes up ‹whatever fasts she broke›. Or if either one ‹broke her fast out of› fear for her child, ‹she must make it up› and whoever provides for the child must give food ‹which is one *mudd* [0.51 liters] of wheat or half a *sāʿ* [2.04 liters] of something else, for each day. He can give all of the food to a single poor person, all at once›.

Whoever loses consciousness or is insane the entirety of the day: his fast is not valid, and the one who lost consciousness makes it up.

The Intention to Fast

وَلَا يَصِحُّ صَوْمُ فَرْضٍ إِلَّا بِنِيَّةٍ مُعَيَّنَةٍ بِجُزْءٍ مِنْ ٱللَّيْلِ، وَيَصِحُّ نَفْلٌ مِمَّنْ لَمْ يَفْعَلْ مُفْسِدًا بِنِيَّةٍ نَهَارًا مُطْلَقًا.

An obligatory [*farḍ*] fast is not valid except with a specific intention during some part of the night ‹by believing himself to be fasting for Ramadan, making it up, performing a vowed fast, or a fast that is an expiatory fast›. Voluntary fasts are valid from someone who has not done something to invalidate it with an intention made during the day, categorically [*muṭlaqan*] ‹whether the intention is before noon or after it›.

Fast Invalidators

(فَصْلٌ) وَمَنْ أَدْخَلَ إِلَى جَوْفِهِ، أَوْ مُجَوَّفٍ فِي جَسَدِهِ كَدِمَاغٍ وَحَلْقٍ شَيْئًا مِنْ أَيِّ مَوْضِعٍ كَانَ غَيْرَ إِحْلِيلِهِ أَوْ اِبْتَلَعَ نُخَامَةً بَعْدَ وُصُولِهَا إِلَى فَمِهِ أَوْ اسْتَقَاءَ فَقَاءَ، أَوْ

اِسْتَمْنَى، أَوْ بَاشَرَ دُونَ اَلْفَرْجِ فَأَمْنَى، أَوْ أَمْذَى أَوْ كَرَّرَ اَلنَّظَرَ فَأَمْنَى، أَوْ نَوَى اَلْإِفْطَارَ، أَوْ حَجَمَ، أَوْ اِحْتَجَمَ عَامِدًا مُخْتَارًا ذَاكِرًا لِصَوْمِهِ أَفْطَرَ، لَا إِنْ فَكَّرَ فَأَنْزَلَ، أَوْ دَخَلَ مَاءُ مَضْمَضَةٍ أَوْ اِسْتِنْشَاقٍ حَلْقَهُ، وَلَوْ بَالَغَ أَوْ زَادَ عَلَى ثَلَاثٍ.

Whoever inserts anything into his body or a body cavity (like the brain and throat ‹and the inside of the vagina or similar things that lead to the stomach›), from any location other than the urethra; swallows mucus after it reaches his mouth; induces vomit and vomits; ejaculates or releases pre-ejaculate [*madhī*] from masturbation or non-genital rubbing; looks repeatedly and ejaculates; intends to break their fast; is cupped or cups someone else – deliberately, voluntarily, and remembering the fast – has broken [the fast] ‹even if he is unaware that it is unlawful›. But ‹the fast is› not ‹broken› if thought leads to orgasm, or water from rinsing the mouth or nostrils enters his throat – even if he did so vigorously, or exceeded three ‹times, even if not done for purification›.

وَمَنْ جَامَعَ بِرَمَضَانَ نَهَارًا بِلَا عُذْرِ شَبَقٍ وَنَحْوِهِ فَعَلَيْهِ اَلْقَضَاءُ وَالْكَفَّارَةُ مُطْلَقًا وَلَا كَفَّارَةَ عَلَيْهَا مَعَ اَلْعُذْرِ: كَنَوْمٍ، وَإِكْرَاهٍ، وَنِسْيَانٍ وَجَهْلٍ، وَعَلَيْهَا الْقَضَاءُ، وَهِيَ عِتْقُ رَقَبَةٍ، فَإِنْ لَمْ يَجِدْ فَصِيَامُ شَهْرَيْنِ مُتَتَابِعَيْنِ، فَإِنْ لَمْ يَسْتَطِعْ فَإِطْعَامُ سِتِّينَ مِسْكِينًا، فَإِنْ لَمْ يَجِدْ سَقَطَتْ.

Whoever has intercourse in the daytime of Ramadan without overwhelming need for sex and the like ‹e.g., a sickness that is improved through sex› must make it up and give an expiation, categorically [*muṭlaqan*] ‹whether ignorant, forgetful, mistaken – such as someone who thought it was night and it turned out to be day, compelled or participated voluntarily›. No expiation is required ‹of the woman› when she has an excuse, such as sleeping, compulsion, forgetfulness, and ignorance. But she must make it up.

The expiation is freeing a slave or, in its absence, fasting consecutively for two months. Whoever is unable ‹to fast› can give food to sixty poor. In their absence, the obligation is dropped.

وَكُرِهَ أَنْ يَجْمَعَ رِيقَهُ فَيَبْتَلِعَهُ، وَذَوْقُ طَعَامٍ، وَمَضْغُ عِلْكٍ لَا يَتَحَلَّلُ، وَإِنْ وَجَدَ طَعْمَهُمَا فِي حَلْقِهِ أَفْطَرَ، وَالْقُبْلَةُ وَنَحْوِهَا مِمَّنْ تُحَرِّكُ شَهْوَتَهُ.

وَيَحْرُمُ إِنْ ظَنَّ إِنْزَالاً، وَمَضْغُ عِلْكٍ يَتَحَلَّلُ، [وَكَذِبٌ] وَغِيْبَةٌ، وَنَمِيمَةٌ وَشَتْمٌ وَنَحْوُهُ بِتَأَكُّدٍ.

It is offensive to gather one's spit and then swallow it; to taste food or suck on mastic that does not dissolve – and the fast is invalid if the taste reaches the throat.

Kissing and its like ‹e.g., hugging, touching, and repeatedly looking; are offensive› for someone who will be aroused. They are unlawful if he thinks he will orgasm.

‹It is unlawful› to suck mastic that dissolves ‹even if one does not swallow one's saliva›.

Lying, gossiping, tale-bearing, abusing, and the like ‹e.g., extremely ugly sin and disobedience› are emphatically ‹unlawful›.

وَسُنَّ تَعْجِيلُ فِطْرٍ، وَتَأْخِيرُ سُحُورٍ وَقَوْلُ مَا وَرَدَ عِنْدَ فِطْرٍ وَتُتَابِعُ اَلْقَضَاءَ فَوْرًا وَحَرُمَ تَأْخِيرُهُ إِلَى آخِرٍ بِلَا عُذْرٍ، فَإِنْ فَعَلَ وَجَبَ مَعَ اَلْقَضَاءِ إِطْعَامُ مِسْكِينٍ عَنْ كُلِّ يَوْمٍ، وَإِنْ مَاتَ اَلْمُفَرِّطُ وَلَوْ قَبْلَ آخَرَ أُطْعِمَ عَنْهُ كَذَلِكَ مِنْ رَأْسِ مَالِهِ، وَلَا يُصَامُ، وَإِنْ كَانَ عَلَى اَلْمَيِّتِ نَذْرٌ مِنْ حَجٍّ، أَوْ صَوْمٍ، أَوْ صَلَاةٍ، أَوْ نَحْوِهَا سُنَّ لِوَلِيِّهِ قَضَاؤُهُ وَمَعَ تَرِكَةٍ يَجِبُ، لَا مُبَاشَرَةُ وَلِيٍّ.

It is recommended to hasten breaking one's fast and to delay one's pre-fast meal; to say what has been narrated when breaking fast:

> ‹"*Allāhuma laka ṣumtu, wa ʿalā rizqika afṭartu, subḥānaka Llāhumma wa bi-ḥamdika, Allāhumma taqabbal minnī, innaka anta s-samīʿu l-alīm*"
>
> ("O Allah, for your sake I fasted, and upon your sustenance I break it. O Allah, accept it from me. Indeed, you are the All-Hearing, All-Knowing")›;

to make up fasts consecutively and immediately.

It is unlawful to delay making up fasts without excuse. If one delays excessively, then – along with the make up – one must feed one poor person for each day. If someone breaking his fast dies – even if before another ‹Ramadan› – food is also given on his behalf from the top of his estate [i.e. before the estate is distributed to inheritors] and fasting is not performed on his behalf.

If someone dies having vowed to perform Hajj, a fast, a prayer, or the like ‹e.g., circumambulation or a vowed spiritual retreat [*iʿtikāf*]›, it is recommended for his guardian to make it up. When there is an estate, it must be done, though the guardian does not have to perform it himself.

Recommended Fasts

(فَصْلٌ) يُسَنُّ صَوْمُ أَيَّامِ اَلْبِيضِ وَالْخَمِيسِ وَالِاثْنَيْنِ، وَسِتٍّ مِنْ شَوَّالٍ، وَشَهْرِ اَللهِ اَلْمُحَرَّمِ، وَآكَدُهُ اَلْعَاشِرُ ثُمَّ اَلتَّاسِعُ، وَتِسْعِ ذِي اَلْحِجَّةِ، وَآكَدُهُ يَوْمُ عَرَفَةَ لِغَيْرِ حَاجٍّ بِهَا.

It is recommended to fast the White Days ‹the 13–15th of every lunar month›; Thursdays; Mondays; six days from Shawwāl; Allah's month Muḥarram (with the tenth and then the ninth being more emphatic); the nine days from the start of Dhi l-Ḥijjah (with the Day of ʿArafah being most emphatic) for individuals not performing Hajj.

وَأَفْضَلُ اَلصِّيَامِ صَوْمُ يَوْمٍ وَفِطْرُ يَوْمٍ، وَكُرِهَ إِفْرَادُ رَجَبٍ وَالْجُمُعَةِ وَالسَّبْتِ وَالشَّكِّ، وَكُلِّ عِيدٍ لِلْكُفَّارِ، وَتَقَدُّمُ رَمَضَانَ بِيَوْمٍ أَوْ بِيَوْمَيْنِ مَا لَمْ يُوَافِقْ عَادَةً فِي اَلْكُلِّ.

The best fast is ‹the fast of Dāwūd (*ʿalayhi s-salām*):› fasting one day and breaking fast the next. It is offensive to single out ‹the entire month of› Rajab, Friday, Saturday, the Day of Doubt ‹the 30th day of Shaʿban when there is something affecting visibility, such as clouds›, every celebration of disbelievers; and fasting one or two days before Ramadan. All [are offensive] so long as the fast does not match one's habit.

وَحَرُمَ صَوْمُ اَلْعِيدَيْنِ مُطْلَقًا، وَأَيَّامُ اَلتَّشْرِيقِ إِلَّا عَنْ دَمِ مُتْعَةٍ وَقِرَانٍ.

It is unlawful to fast the two days of Eid, categorically [*muṭlaqan*] ‹whether the fast is obligatory or voluntary – and it is invalid›, and the Days of Tashrīq [11–13 Dhi l-Ḥijjah] (unless making a blood sacrifice for performing Umrah and then Hajj or performing them both together).

وَمَنْ دَخَلَ فِي فَرْضٍ مُوَسَّعٍ حَرُمَ قَطْعُهُ بِلَا عُذْرٍ أَوْ نَفْلٍ غَيْرَ حَجٍّ وَعُمْرَةٍ كُرِهَ بِلَا عُذْرٍ.

It is unlawful to interrupt an obligatory [*farḍ*] act which allows for multiple performances within its valid time [*farḍ muwassaʿ*] ‹e.g., making up Ramadan before the next one, performing a prayer at the beginning of its time› without an excuse once one begins it. It is offensive to interrupt a voluntary act other than Hajj or Umrah without an excuse.

Spiritual Retreat

(فَصْلٌ) وَالْاعْتِكَافُ سُنَّةٌ، وَلَا يَصِحُّ مِمَّنْ تَلْزَمُهُ اَلْجَمَاعَةُ إِلَّا فِي مَسْجِدٍ تُقَامُ فِيهِ إِنْ أَتَى عَلَيْهِ صَلَاةٌ، وَشُرِطَ لَهُ طَهَارَةٌ مِمَّا يُوجِبُ غُسْلاً.

Spiritual Retreat [*iʿtikāf*] is recommended. It is not valid from someone who is required to attend congregational prayers except in a mosque where a congregation is held if a prayer will occur [during the time of his retreat].

A condition for it[s performance] is that one is free of anything requiring performing the purificatory bath ‹e.g, menstruation or lochia›.

وَإِنْ نَذَرَهُ أَوْ اَلصَّلَاةَ فِي مَسْجِدٍ غَيْرَ اَلثَّلَاثَةِ - فَلَهُ فِعْلُهُ فِي غَيْرِهِ، وفي أَحَدِهَا فَلَهُ فِعْلُهُ فِيهِ، وَفِي اَلْأَفْضَلِ، وَأَفْضَلُهَا اَلْمَسْجِدُ اَلْحَرَامُ، ثُمَّ مَسْجِدُ النَّبِيِّ-عَلَيْهِ اَلسَّلَامُ - [فَالْأَقْصَى].

If one vows to perform spiritual retreat or prayer in a mosque other than the three [al-Masjid al-Ḥarām in Mecca, the Mosque of the Prophet ﷺ in Medina, and al-Aqṣā in Jerusalem], one can perform it in another mosque. But if one vows it in one of those three, one must perform it there or in a superior mosque. The most superior is al-Masjid al-Ḥarām, then the Mosque of the Prophet ﷺ, and then al-Aqṣā.

وَلَا يَخْرُجُ مَنْ اِعْتَكَفَ مَنْذُورًا مُتَتَابِعًا إِلَّا لِمَا لَا بُدَّ مِنْهُ وَلَا يَعُودُ مَرِيضًا، وَلَا يَشْهَدُ جِنَازَةً إِلَّا بِشَرْطٍ.

One does not exit from a spiritual retreat that one has vowed to perform consecutively except for something unavoidable ‹e.g., fetching his own food and drink when no one will bring it for him, vomiting, washing away filth, relieving oneself, performing an obligatory ablution (even if for a prayer before its time has entered)›. He does not visit someone who is sick nor attend a funeral unless it was stipulated ‹though it is not valid to stipulate exiting for trade or whenever one wants›.

وَوَطْءُ اَلْفَرْجِ يُفْسِدُهُ، وَكَذَا إِنْزَالٌ بِمُبَاشَرَةٍ، وَيَلْزَمُ لِإِفْسَادِهِ كَفَّارَةُ يَمِينٍ.

Intercourse spoils it. So does ejaculating from foreplay.

An expiation for oath breaking is required for spoiling ‹a spiritual retreat one had vowed to perform›.

وَسُنَّ اِشْتِغَالُهُ بِالْقُرَبِ، وَاجْتِنَابُ مَا لَا يَعْنِيهِ.

It is recommended to busy oneself with acts of worship and to avoid whatever does not concern one ‹e.g., debating, arguing, and frequent speech›.

6

PILGRIMAGE

كِتَابُ الْحَجِّ

يَجِبَانِ عَلَى ٱلْمُسْلِمِ ٱلْحُرِّ ٱلْمُكَلَّفِ ٱلْمُسْتَطِيعِ فِي ٱلْعُمْرِ مَرَّةً عَلَى ٱلْفَوْرِ، فَإِنْ زَالَ مَانِعُ حَجٍّ بِعَرَفَةَ وَعُمْرَةٍ قَبْلَ طَوَافِهَا وَفُعِلَا إِذَنْ وَقَعَا فَرْضًا.

Hajj and Umrah are both obligatory ‹when five conditions are met›

‹1–2› for Muslims who are free;

‹3–4› responsible ‹i.e., mature and sane›; and,

‹5› able.

‹They are obligatory› once in a lifetime, and ‹once the conditions for its obligation have been fulfilled, to leave for it› immediately ‹provided the way is safe›.

If something preventing Hajj ceases to do so ‹e.g., a youth matures, a slave is freed, consciousness is regained› at ʿArafah ‹or afterward if one returns and stands on it in time›, or something preventing Umrah ‹ends, e.g., a disbeliever enters Islam› before the Circumambulation for Umrah and they ‹Hajj and Umrah› are performed: in that case they take place as the obligatory [*farḍ*] act.

وَإِنْ عَجَزَ لِكِبَرٍ أَوْ مَرَضٍ لَا يُرْجَى بُرْؤُهُ لَزِمَهُ أَنْ يُقِيمَ مَنْ يَحُجُّ عَنْهُ وَيَعْتَمِرُ مِنْ حَيْثُ وَجَبَا، وَيُجْزِآنِهِ مَا لَمْ يَبْرَأْ قَبْلَ إِحْرَامِ نَائِبٍ.

If one is unable due to old age or a chronic illness, one is required to support someone to perform Hajj and Umrah on one's behalf from wherever the rites became obligatory. The ‹substitute's› performances of Hajj and Umrah suffice him so long as he does not recover before his substitute's entry into the state of pilgrimage [*iḥrām*].

وَشُرِطَ لِامْرَأَةٍ مَحْرَمٌ أَيْضًا، فَإِنْ أَيِسَتْ مِنْهُ اسْتَنَابَتْ.

Additionally, a condition a woman [being obligated] is having a close male relative [*maḥram*]. If she loses hope ‹of having a close relative›, she picks someone to perform it as her substitute.

وَإِنْ مَاتَ مَنْ لَزِمَاهُ أُخْرِجَا مِنْ تَرِكَتِهِ.

If someone required to perform Hajj or Umrah dies, it ‹whatever is needed to do so› is taken from his estate.

وَسُنَّ لِمُرِيدِ إِحْرَامٍ غُسْلٌ أَوْ تَيَمُّمٌ لِعُذْرٍ، وَتَنَظُّفٌ، وَتَطَيُّبٌ فِي بَدَنٍ، وَكُرِهَ فِي ثَوْبٍ، وَإِحْرَامٌ بِإِزَارٍ وَرِدَاءٍ أَبْيَضَيْنِ عَقِبَ فَرِيضَةٍ أَوْ رَكْعَتَيْنِ فِي غَيْرِ وَقْتِ نَهْيٍ.

It is recommended for someone wishing to enter the state of pilgrimage to make the purificatory bath or, if excused, dry ablution; to clean themselves ‹e.g., to shave their pubic hair, pluck armpit hair, crop their mustache, pare their nails, remove offensive odors›; to apply perfume to their body (it being offensive to apply it to the clothes).

‹It is recommended› to enter the state of pilgrimage wearing a waist wrapper [*izār*] and shawl [*ridāʾ*] that are white – after praying an obligatory prayer, or ‹after› two prayer-cycles when not in a time in which prayer is prohibited.

وَنِيَّتُهُ شَرْطٌ، وَالِاشْتِرَاطُ فِيهِ سُنَّةٌ.

Intending to enter the state of pilgrimage is a condition [for its validity]. Stipulating [a release in the event something bars one from completing the pilgrimage] is recommended ‹e.g., "O Allah, I intend to perform such-and-such, so make it easy for me and accept it from me. If anything restrains me then my release [from pilgrimage] is wherever I am restrained"›.

وَأَفْضَلُ اَلْأَنْسَاكِ اَلتَّمَتُّعِ، وَهُوَ أَنْ يُحْرِمَ بِعُمْرَةٍ فِي أَشْهُرِ اَلْحَجِّ وَيَفْرُغَ مِنْهَا، ثُمَّ بِهِ فِي عَامِهِ.

The superior way to perform the rites is *tamattuʿ*. It is when one enters the state of pilgrimage to perform Umrah during the months of Hajj, completes it, and then enters the state of pilgrimage to perform Hajj during the same year.

ثُمَّ اَلْإِفْرَادُ وَهُوَ أَنْ يُحْرِمَ بِحَجٍّ ثُمَّ بِعُمْرَةٍ بَعْدَ فَرَاغِهِ مِنْهُ. وَالْقِرَانُ أَنْ يُحْرِمَ بِهِمَا مَعًا أَوْ بِهَا ثُمَّ يُدْخِلَهُ عَلَيْهَا قَبْلَ اَلشُّرُوعِ فِي طَوَافِهَا.

The next superior way is *ifrād*. It is when one enters the state of pilgrimage to perform Hajj and then, upon its completion, enters the state of pilgrimage to perform Umrah.

Qirān is when one enters the state of pilgrimage to perform both rites together, or to perform Umrah and then appends Hajj before making Umrah's Circumambulation.

وَعَلَى كُلٍّ مِنْ مُتَمَتِّعٍ وَقَارِنٍ -إِذَا كَانَ أُفُقِيًّا- دَمُ نُسُكٍ بِشَرْطِهِ.

Everyone who performs *tamattuʿ* and *qirān* who comes from afar [*ufuqiyyan*] must make a blood sacrifice [*dam nusuk*] (according to its conditions).

وَإِنْ حَاضَتْ مُتَمَتِّعَةٌ فَخَشِيَتْ فَوَاتَ اَلْحَجِّ أَحْرَمَتْ بِهِ وَصَارَتْ قَارِنَةً.

If a woman performing *tamattuʿ* menstruates ‹or has lochia before making Umrah's obligatory circumambulation› and she fears missing Hajj, she enters the state of pilgrimage for Hajj and performs *qirān*.

وَتُسَنُّ ٱلتَّلْبِيَةُ، وَتَتَأَكَّدُ إِذَا عَلَا نَشْزًا أَوْ هَبَطَ وَادِيًا أَوْ صَلَّى مَكْتُوبَةً أَوْ أَقْبَلَ لَيْلٌ أَوْ نَهَارٌ أَوْ ٱلْتَقَتِ الرِّفَاقُ أَوْ رَكِبَ أَوْ نَزَلَ أَوْ سَمِعَ مُلَبِّيًا أَوْ رَأَى الْبَيْتَ أَوْ فَعَلَ مَحْظُورًا نَاسِيًا

It is recommended to say the *talbiyah*, with it being emphasized whenever one has crested a ridge [*nushuzan*], descended into a valley, prayed an obligatory prayer, [or when] night or day approaches, looks to his companions, mounts or alights [from his transport], hears someone saying the *talbiyah*, or forgetfully does something proscribed ‹when he remembers›.

وَكُرِهَ إِحْرَامٌ قَبْلَ مِيقَاتٍ، وَبِحَجٍّ قَبْلَ أَشْهُرِهِ.

It is offensive to enter the state of pilgrimage [*iḥrām*] before its appointed places of entry [*mīqāt*], and to enter Hajj before its appointed months.

The Mīqāt and Things Unlawful During Pilgrimage

(فَصْلٌ) وَمِيقَاتُ أَهْلِ ٱلْمَدِينَةِ الْحُلَيْفَةُ، وَالشَّامِ وَمِصْرَ وَٱلْمَغْرِبِ ٱلْجُحْفَةُ وَالْيَمَنِ يَلَمْلَمَ، وَنَجْدٍ قَرْنٌ وَٱلْمَشْرِقِ ذَاتُ عِرْقٍ.

Al-Ḥulayfah is the designated point of entry for the people of Medina; al-Juḥfah is for the Levant, Egypt, and the west; Yalamlam is for Yemen; Qarn is for Najd; and Dhāt ʿIrq is for the east.

وَيُحْرِمُ مِنْ مَكَّةَ لِحَجٍّ مِنْهَا، وَلِعُمْرَةٍ مِنَ ٱلْحِلِّ.

Whoever is in Mecca enters Hajj from it, and Umrah from outside the Sacred Precinct [*al-ḥill*].

وَأَشْهُرُ ٱلْحَجِّ شَوَّالٌ، وَذُو ٱلْقَعْدَةِ وَعَشْرٌ مِنْ ذِي ٱلْحِجَّةِ.

The months for [entering] Hajj are Shawwāl, Dhu l-Qaʿdah, and the [first] ten days of Dhi l-Ḥijjah.

مَحْظُورَاتُ اَلْإِحْرَامِ تِسْعَةٌ: إِزَالَةُ شَعْرٍ، وَتَقْلِيمُ أَظْفَارٍ، وَتَغْطِيَةُ رَأْسِ ذَكَرٍ، وَلَبْسُهُ اَلْمَخِيطَ إِلا سَرَاوِيلَ لِعَدَمِ إِزَارٍ، وَخُفَّيْنِ لِعَدَمِ نَعْلَيْنِ، وَالطِّيبُ، وَقَتْلُ صَيْدِ اَلْبَرِّ وَعَقْدُ نِكَاحٍ، وَجِمَاعٌ، وَمُبَاشَرَةٌ فِيمَا دُونَ فَرْجٍ.

The things proscribed while in the state of pilgrimage are nine:
‹1› removing hair;
‹2› paring the nails;
‹3–4› for a man to cover his head or wear sewn garments with the exception of trousers in the absence of an *izār* or *khuff* in the absence of sandals;
‹5› using perfume;
‹6› killing land-based game animals;
‹7› contracting marriage;
‹8› intercourse; and,
‹9› foreplay.

فَفِي أَقَلَّ مِنْ ثَلَاثِ شَعَرَاتٍ وَثَلَاثَةِ أَظْفَارٍ فِي كُلِّ وَاحِدٍ فَأَقَلَّ طَعَامُ مِسْكِينٍ، وَفِي اَلثَّلَاثِ فَأَكْثَرَ دَمٌ، وَفِي تَغْطِيَةِ اَلرَّأْسِ بِلَاصِقٍ وَلُبْسِ مَخِيطٍ وَتَطَيُّبٍ فِي بَدَنٍ، أَوْ ثَوْبٍ، أَوْ شَمٍّ، أَوْ دَهْنٍ اَلْفِدْيَةُ، وَإِنْ قَتَلَ صَيْدًا مَأْكُولاً بَرِّيًّا أَصْلاً فَعَلَيْهِ جَزَاؤُهُ.

For removing less than three hairs or nails, one must feed someone who is poor for each complete or partial ‹hair or nail› removed. For removing three or more ‹hairs or nails›, one must make a blood sacrifice.

For covering the head with something that touches it, wearing sewn garments, applying perfume to the body or clothing or smelling it, and applying oil – one must make a *fidyah* sacrifice.

For killing an edible land-based game animal ‹whether doing so directly or causing it do be done›, one must give its compensation.

وَالْجِمَاعُ قَبْلَ اَلتَّحَلُّلِ اَلْأَوَّلِ فِي حَجٍّ وَقَبْلَ فَرَاغِ سَعْيٍ فِي عُمْرَةٍ مُفْسِدٌ لِنُسُكِهِمَا مُطْلَقًا، وَفِيهِ لِحَجٍّ بَدَنَةٌ، وَلِعُمْرَةٍ شَاةٌ، وَيَمْضِيَانِ فِي فَاسِدِهِ، وَيَقْضِيَانِهِ مُطْلَقًا إِنْ كَانَا مُكَلَّفَيْنِ فَوْرًا، وَإِلَّا بَعْدَ اَلتَّكْلِيفِ، وَحَجَّةِ الإِسْلَامِ فَوْرًا.

Intercourse before the first release [*taḥallul*] during Hajj or before completing Umrah's traversal spoils them both, categorically [*muṭlaqan*] ‹whether one was forgetful, ignorant, compelled, or asleep›. For doing so during Hajj ‹i.e., intercourse before the first release›, one must sacrifice a camel [*badanah*]. For doing so during Umrah ‹before the first release›, one must sacrifice a sheep [*shāh*]. Both must complete their spoiled rites and make them up, categorically [*muṭlaqan*] ‹whether the participant is an adult or minor, penetrator or penetrated; and whether the rite is obligatory or voluntary›. They must make them up immediately if they are legally responsible. Otherwise, they make them up immediately after becoming legally responsible and performing their obligatory Hajj.

وَلَا يَفْسُدُ اَلنّسكُ بِمُبَاشَرَةٍ، وَيَجِبُ بِهَا بَدَنَةٌ إِنْ أَنْزَلَ وَإِلَّا شَاةٌ، وَلَا بِوَطْءٍ فِي حَجٍّ بَعْدَ اَلتَّحَلُّلِ اَلْأَوَّلِ وَقَبْلَ اَلثَّانِي، لَكِنْ يَفْسُدُ اَلْإِحْرَامُ فَيُحْرِمُ مِنَ اَلْحِلِّ لِيَطُوفَ لِلزِّيَارَةِ فِي إِحْرَامٍ صَحِيحٍ، وَيَسْعَى إِنْ لَمْ يَكُنْ سَعَى، وَعَلَيْهِ شَاةٌ.

Foreplay does not invalidate the rites. Sacrificing a camel is obligatory if one orgasms. Otherwise, a sheep is obligatory.

Intercourse during Hajj between the first and second releases [*al-taḥallul al-awwal*, and *al-taḥallul al-thāni*] does not spoil it. However, it does spoil the state of pilgrimage [*al-iḥrām*], so one must [re]enter it from outside the Sacred Precinct [*al-ḥill*] so that they can perform the Visitation Circumambulation while in a sound state of pilgrimage and traverse [between Ṣafā and Marwah] if they had not done so. He must sacrifice a sheep.

وَإِحْرَامُ امْرَأَةٍ كَرَجُلٍ إِلَّا فِي لُبْسِ مَخِيطٍ، وَتَجْتَنِبُ اَلْبُرْقَعَ وَالْقُفَّازَيْنِ وَتَغْطِيَةَ اَلْوَجْهِ، فَإِنْ غَطَّتْهُ بِلَا عُذْرٍ فَدَتْ.

A woman's entry into the state of pilgrimage [*iḥrām*] is like a man's except concerning wearing stitched clothing, avoiding wearing a face-covering [*burqaʿ*] or gloves, and covering her face. If she covers her face without an excuse to do so, she must make an expiation.

Expiations & Compensations

(فَصْلٌ) يُخَيَّرُ بِفِدْيَةِ حَلْقٍ وتَقْلِيمٍ وَتَغْطِيَةِ رَأْسٍ وَطِيبٍ بَيْنَ صِيَامِ ثَلَاثَةِ أَيَّامٍ، أَوْ إِطْعَامِ سِتَّةِ مَسَاكِينَ، كُلِّ مِسْكِينٍ مُدَّ بُرٍّ أَوْ نِصْفَ صَاعِ تَمْرٍ، أَوْ زَبِيبٍ أَوْ شَعِيرٍ، أَوْ ذَبْحِ شَاةٍ.

Expiation mends the following: shaving, paring nails, covering the head, and using perfume. One chooses between fasting three days; giving food to six of the poor, giving each poor individual a *mudd* [0.51 liters] of wheat, or half a *ṣāʿ* [2.04 liters ÷ 2 = 1.02 liters] of dried dates or raisins or barley; or slaughtering a sheep.

وَفِي جَزَاءِ صَيْدٍ بَيْنَ مِثْلِ مِثْلِيٍّ أَوْ تَقْوِيمِهِ بِدَرَاهِمَ يَشْتَرِي بِهَا طَعَامًا يُجْزِيءُ فِي فِطْرَةٍ فَيُطْعِمُ عَنْ كُلِّ مِسْكِينٍ مُدَّ بُرٍّ أَوْ نِصْفَ صَاعٍ مِنْ غَيْرِهِ أَوْ يَصُومُ عَنْ طَعَامِ كُلِّ مِسْكِينٍ يَوْمًا، وَبَيْنَ إِطْعَامٍ أَوْ صِيَامٍ فِي غَيْرِ مِثْلِيٍّ.

For compensation for hunting [or slaughtering a land animal that has an analogous type], one chooses between: [slaughtering] a similar animal; and appraising its value in *dirham*s and then using them to either purchase food appropriate for *zakāt al-fiṭr* which is given to the poor (each individual getting one *mudd* of wheat of half a *ṣāʿ* of non-wheat), or fasting one day in place of each poor person who would have been fed.

When compensating for hunting [or slaughtering a land animal] that does not have an analogous type, one chooses between feeding [the poor], and fasting.

وَإِنْ عَدِمَ مُتَمَتِّعٌ أَوْ قَارِنٌ اَلْهَدْيَ صَامَ ثَلَاثَةَ أَيَّامٍ فِي اَلْحَجِّ، وَالْأَفْضَلُ جَعْلُ آخِرِهَا يَوْمُ عَرَفَةَ، وَسَبْعَةً إِذَا رَجَعَ لِأَهْلِهِ،

وَالْمُحْصَرِ إِذَا لَمْ يَجِدْهُ صَامَ عَشَرَةَ أَيَّامٍ، ثُمَّ حَلَّ،

وَتَسْقُطُ بِنِسْيَانٍ فِي لُبْسٍ، وَطِيبٍ وَتَغْطِيَةِ رَأْسٍ.

Someone performing Umrah and then Hajj the same year [*mutamatiʿ*] or both of them simultaneously [*qārin*] who cannot find a sacrificial animal fasts three days during Hajj (with it being best to make the last day on the Day of ʿArafah) and seven days upon returning to their family.

Someone who is held back [from performing pilgrimage, *muḥṣar*] and does not find a sacrificial animal is to fast ten days, after which he is released [from pilgrim's sanctity].

The expiation for wearing clothing, applying perfume, and covering the head ceases being obligatory by forgetfulness ‹and by ignorance and compulsion›.

وَكُلُّ هَدْيٍ أَوْ طَعَامٍ فَلِمَسَاكِينِ اَلْحَرَمِ، إِلَّا فِدْيَةَ أَذًى وَلُبْسٍ وَنَحْوِهَا، فَحَيْثُ وُجِدَ سَبَبُهَا، وَيُجْزِئُ اَلصَّوْمُ بِكُلِّ مَكَانٍ، وَالدَّمُ شَاةٌ أَوْ سُبُعُ بَدَنَةٍ أَوْ بَقَرَةٍ.

All sacrificed animals and expiatory food belong to the poor within the Sacred Precinct – except for the expiation for annoyances, wearing clothing, and the like ‹e.g., perfume, foreplay without orgasm›, as they are owed wherever their cause occurs.

Fasting suffices wherever done.

The blood sacrifice is either a sheep, or one-seventh of a camel or a cow.

وَيُرْجَعُ فِي جَزَاءِ اَلصَّيْدِ إِلَى مَا قَضَتْ فِيهِ اَلصَّحَابَةُ، وَفِيمَا لَمْ تَقْضِ فِيهِ إِلَى قَوْلِ عَدْلَيْنِ خَبِيرَيْنِ، وَمَا لَا مِثْلَ لَهُ تَجِبُ قِيمَتُهُ مَكَانَهُ.

For compensation for hunting, one returns to the judgments of the Companions [may Allah be pleased with them]. If they did not adjudicate ‹a particular type of animal that has a likeness›, then one returns to two upright experts. And for whatever has no likeness, one returns to its value at its location.

وَحَرُمَ مُطْلَقًا صَيْدُ حَرَمِ مَكَّةَ، وَقَطْعُ شَجَرِهِ وَحَشِيشِهِ إِلَّا ٱلْإِذْخِرَ وَفِيهِ ٱلْجَزَاءُ، وَصَيْدُ حَرَمِ ٱلْمَدِينَةِ، وَقَطْعُ شَجَرِهِ وَحَشِيشِهِ لِغَيْرِ حَاجَةِ عَلَفٍ وَقَتَبٍ وَنَحْوِهِمَا وَلَا جَزَاءَ.

Hunting within the Sacred Precinct of Mecca is forbidden categorically [*muṭlaqan*] ‹for pilgrims and non-pilgrims›.

‹It is forbidden› to cut its trees and grass – except for *idhkhir* [a certain kind of plant, said to be sweet rush]. Compensation is owed for it.

‹It is forbidden› to hunt within the Sacred Precinct of Medina, and to cut its trees and grass without needing them for fodder, camel saddles, and their like ‹e.g., things needed for cultivation and travel›. No compensation is owed for it.

Entering Mecca

(بَابٌ) يَسُنُّ نَهَارًا مِنْ أَعْلَاهَا، وَٱلْمَسْجِدُ مِنْ بَابِ أَبِي شَيْبَةَ، فَإِذَا رَأَى ٱلْبَيْتَ رَفَعَ يَدَهُ وَقَالَ مَا وَرَدَ، ثُمَّ طَافَ مُضْطَبِعًا لِلْعُمْرَةِ ٱلْمُعْتَمِرُ، وَلِلْقُدُومِ غَيْرُهُ، وَيَسْتَلِمُ ٱلْحَجَرَ ٱلْأَسْوَدَ وَيُقَبِّلُهُ، فَإِنْ شَقَّ أَشَارَ إِلَيْهِ، وَيَقُولُ مَا وَرَدَ، وَيَرْمُلُ ٱلْأُفُقِيُّ فِي هَذَا ٱلطَّوَافِ، فَإِذَا فَرَغَ صَلَّى رَكْعَتَيْنِ خَلْفَ ٱلْمَقَامِ ثُمَّ يَسْتَلِمُ ٱلْحَجَرَ ٱلْأَسْوَدَ وَيَخْرُجُ إِلَى ٱلصَّفَا مِنْ بَابِهِ فَيَرْقَاهُ حَتَّى يَرَى ٱلْبَيْتَ، فَيُكَبِّرُ ثَلَاثًا وَيَقُولُ مَا وَرَدَ، ثُمَّ يَنْزِلُ مَاشِيًا إِلَى ٱلْعَلَمِ ٱلْأَوَّلِ فَيَسْعَى شَدِيدًا إِلَى ٱلْآخَرِ، ثُمَّ يَمْشِي وَيَرْقَى إِلَى ٱلْمَرْوَةِ، وَيَقُولُ مَا قَالَهُ عَلَى ٱلصَّفَا، ثُمَّ يَنْزِلُ فَيَمْشِي فِي مَوْضِعِ مَشْيِهِ وَيَسْعَى فِي مَوْضِعِ سَعْيِهِ إِلَى ٱلصَّفَا، يَفْعَلُهُ سَبْعًا، وَيَحْسِبُ ذَهَابَهُ وَرُجُوعَهُ.

It is recommended to enter Mecca during the day from its highest point ‹at Thaniyah Kadā', later known as al-Maʿlāh Gate›, and to enter the Mosque from Banī Shaybah Gate. When one sees the House, one raises the hands and says what was transmitted

‹*"Allāhumma anta s-salāmu wa minka s-salām, ḥayyinā rabbanā bi-s-salām"*

("O Allah, You are Peace, the Source of Peace; O Lord resurrect us in peace"),

"Allāhumma zid hādha l-bayta taʿẓīman wa tashrīfan wa takrīman wa mahābbatan wa birran wa zid man ʿaẓẓamahu wa sharrafahu taʿẓīman wa tashrīfan wa takrīman wa mahābatan wa birran"

("O Allah, increase this house in reverence, nobility, honor, dignity, and piety. Increase the reverence, honor, nobility, honor, dignity, and piety of those who revere and honor it."),

"Al-ḥamdu li-Llāhi rabbi l-ʿālamin kathīran kamā huwa ahluhu, wa mā yanbaghī li-karami wajhihi, wa ʿizzi jalālihi, wa-l-ḥamdu li-Llāhi l-ladhī ballaghanī baytahu, wa ra'ānī li-dhālika ahlan. Al-Ḥamdu li-Llāhi ʿalā kulli ḥālin, Allāhumma innaka daʿawta ilā ḥajji baytika l-ḥarām, wa qad ji'tuka li-dhālika, Allāhumma taqabbal minnī, wa-ʿfu ʿannī, wa aṣliḥ lī sha'nī kullahu, lā ilāha illā anta"

("Praise is due to Allah, Lord of the worlds, copiously just as befits Him and whatever should be due to His noble Face, the strength of His Glory. Praise is due to Allah Who brought me to His house and saw me fit for it. And praise is due to Allah in all circumstances. O Allah, You have called [Your servants] to make pilgrimage to Your inviolable house, and I have come to You for that.

O Allah, accept it from me, grant me respite, rectify all of my affairs, there is no god but You")›.

One then circumambulates with the middle of one's mantle under the right shoulder [*muḍṭabiʿan*]. Someone making Umrah intends the Umrah Circumambulation; others intend making the Arrival Circumambulation. One faces the Black Stone and kisses it (if kissing it is difficult, one points to it), and says what was transmitted

‹"*bi-smi Llāh, wa-Llāhu akbar, Allāhumma īmānan bika, wa taṣdīqan bi-kitābika, wa wafā'an bi-ʿahdika, wa-tibāʿan li-sunnati nabiyyika Muḥammad* ﷺ"

("In the name of Allah. Allah is most great! O Allah, out of faith in You, affirming Your Book, fulfilling Your covenant, following the Sunnah of Your Prophet Muḥammad ﷺ")

– each time›. Someone coming from afar jogs [*yarmul*] during this Circumambulation. When finished, one prays two prayer-cycles behind the Station ‹of Ibrāhīm›. Then one touches the Black Stone and exits to Ṣafā from its gate, ascends it until one sees the House, says "*Allāhu akbar*" three times, and then what was transmitted

‹"*lā ilāha illa Llāhu waḥdahu lā sharīka lahu, lahu l-mulku, wa lahu l-ḥamdu, yuḥyī wa yumīt, wa huwa ḥayyun lā yamūt, bi-yadihi l-khayr wa huwa ʿalā kulli shay'in qadīr, lā ilāha illa Llāhu waḥdahu lā sharīka lahu, ṣadaqa waʿdahu, wa naṣara ʿabdahu wa hazama l-aḥzāba waḥdahu*"

("There is no god but Allah alone, without partner. His is the dominion, His the praise. He gives life and causes to die, He is alive and never dies, all good is in His hand, and He has power over everything. There is no god but Allah alone, without partner. He kept His promise, gave His slave the victory, and routed the Confederates alone")

– three times, after which one supplicates›. One then descends, walking to the first marker and then walks quickly to the other ‹marker›. One then walks, ascends Marwah, and says what one said on Ṣafā. One then descends, walking where one had [previously] walked, walking quickly where one had [previously] walked quickly, up until reaching Ṣafā. One does the above seven times, counting his departure ‹as a traversal› and his return ‹as a traversal›.

وَيَتَحَلَّلُ مُتَمَتِّعٌ لَا هَدْيَ مَعَهُ بِتَقْصِيرِ شِعْرِهِ، وَمَنْ مَعَهُ هَدْيٌ إِذَا حَجَّ.

Someone performing ʿUrmah and then Hajj in the same year [*mutamattiʿ*] who does not have a sacrificial animal is released by trimming his hair. Someone who does have a sacrificial animal is released when he has performed Hajj.

وَالْمُتَمَتِّعِ يَقْطَعُ اَلتَّلْبِيَةَ إِذَا أَخَذَ فِي اَلطَّوَافِ.

Someone performing Umrah and then Hajj in the same year [*mutamattiʿ*] stops chanting "*Labbayk Allāhumma labbayk...*" when beginning Circumambulation.

How to Perform Hajj and Umrah

(فَصْلٌ) يُسَنُّ لِمُحِلٍّ بِمَكَّةَ اَلْإِحْرَامُ بِالْحَجِّ يَوْمَ اَلتَّرْوِيَةِ وَالْمَبِيتُ بِمِنًى، فَإِذَا طَلَعَتِ اَلشَّمْسُ سَارَ إِلَى عَرَفَةَ، وَكُلُّهَا مَوْقِفٌ إِلَّا بَطْنَ عُرَنَةَ وَجَمَعَ فِيهَا بَيْنَ اَلظُّهْرِ وَالْعَصْرِ تَقْدِيمًا، وَأَكْثَرَ اَلدُّعَاءَ مِمَّا وَرَدَ.

It is recommended for someone present in Mecca to initiate Hajj on Yaum al-Tarwiyah ‹the 8th of Dhi l-Ḥijjah› and to spend the night in Minā. When the sun rises, one travels to ʿArafah. All of ʿArafah is a place for standing, save Baṭn ʿUranah. At ʿArafah, one joins the Noon and Afternoon Prayers in the time of the Noon Prayer. One makes frequent supplication using the ones that were transmitted

‹"*Lā ilāha illa Llāhu waḥdahu lā sharīka lahu, lahu l-mulku wa lahu l-ḥamdu yuḥyī wa yumīt wa huwa ḥayyun lā yamūt, bi-yadihi l-khayr wa huwa ʿalā kulli shayʾin qadīr. Allāhumma-jʿal fī qalbī nūran wa fī baṣarī nūran wa fī samʿī nūran wa yassir lī amrī*"

("There is no god but Allah alone, without partner. His is the dominion, His the praise. He gives life and causes to die, He is alive and never dies, all good is in His hand, and He has power over everything. O Allah, place light in my heart, light in my sight, light in my hearing, and facilitate my affairs")›.

وَوَقْتُ اَلْوُقُوفِ: مِنْ فَجْرِ عَرَفَةَ إِلَى فَجْرِ اَلنَّحْرِ، ثُمَّ يَدْفَعُ بَعْدَ اَلْغُرُوبِ إِلَى اَلْمُزْدَلِفَةَ بِسَكِينَةٍ وَيَجْمَعُ فِيهَا بَيْنَ العِشَاءَيْنِ تَأْخِيرًا وَيَبِيتُ بِهَا، فَإِذَا صَلَّى اَلصُّبْحَ أَتَى اَلْمَشْعَرَ اَلْحَرَامَ، فَرَقَاهُ وَوَقَفَ عِنْدَهُ، وَحَمِدَ اَللهَ وَكَبَّرَ وَقَرَأَ: ﴿فَإِذَا أَفَضْتُمْ مِنْ عَرَفَاتٍ﴾ (اَلْبَقَرَةِ: ١٩٨-١٩٩) اَلْآيَتَيْنِ.

The time for standing is from dawn on the Day of ʿArafah up until dawn on the Day of Sacrifice [*yaum al-naḥr*]. After sunset, one goes to Muzdalifah, where one joins Sunset and Night Prayers (in the time of the latter). One stays the night there. When one prays Dawn Prayer one goes to [the hill of] al-Mashʿar al-Ḥarām and ascends it. One stands there, says "*Al-Ḥamdu lillāh, Allāhu akbar*" and recites "But when you depart from ʿArafāt, remember Allah at al-Mashʿar al-Ḥarām. And remember Him, as He has guided you, for indeed, you were before that among those astray. Then depart from the place from where [all] the people depart and ask forgiveness of Allah. Indeed, Allah is Forgiving and Merciful" (Quran, 2:198–99).

وَيَدْعُو حَتَّى يُسْفِرَ، ثُمَّ يَدْفَعُ إِلَى مِنَى، فَإِذَا بَلَغَ مُحَسِّرًا أَسْرَعَ رَمْيَةَ حَجَرٍ، وَأَخَذَ حَصَى اَلْجِمَارَ سَبْعِينَ أَكْبَرَ مِنْ اَلْحِمِّصِ وَدُونَ اَلْبُنْدُقِ، فَيَرْمِي جَمْرَةَ اَلْعَقَبَةِ (وَحْدَهَا)

بِسَبْعٍ، يَرْفَعُ يُمْنَاهُ حَتَّى يُرَى بَيَاضُ إِبْطِهِ، وَيُكَبِّرُ مَعَ كُلِّ حَصَاةٍ، ثُمَّ يَنْحَرُ، وَيَحْلِقُ، أَوْ يُقَصِّرُ مِنْ جَمِيعِ شَعْرِهِ، وَالْمَرْأَةُ قَدْرَ أُنْمُلَةٍ ثُمَّ قَدْ حَلَّ لَهُ كُلُّ شَيْءٍ إِلَّا اَلنِّسَاءَ ثُمَّ يُفِيضُ إِلَى مَكَّةَ

One supplicates until light and then goes to Minā. When he arrives at Muḥassir ‹a valley between Muzdalifah and Minā›, he hastens to throw [pebbles] at the pillar. He takes seventy pebbles for [throwing at] the pillars; they are larger than chickpeas but smaller than hazelnuts [*bunduq*]. He throws at Jamrata l-ʿAqabat alone with seven pebbles, right arm raised until the white of the armpit is visible; with each pebble one says "*Allāhu akbar*" ‹and says, "*Allāhumma jʿalhu ḥajjan mabrūran wa dhibḥan maghfūran wa sayʿan mashkūran*" ("O Allah, make it a pious Hajj, a sacrifice [for which one is] forgiven, and rewarded effort")›. One then slaughters one's sacrifice and either shaves or trims all of one's hair – though a woman trims only a fingertip's amount. Thereupon, everything [that was unlawful during pilgrimage] becomes lawful ‹such as perfume and the like› except for ‹intercourse, foreplay, and the like with› women. One then goes forth to Mecca.

فَيَطُوفُ طَوَافَ الزِّيَارَةِ الَّذِي هُوَ رُكْنٌ ثُمَّ يَسْعَى إِنْ لَمْ يَكُنْ سَعَى وَقَدْ حَلَّ لَهُ كُلُّ شَيْءٍ.

One then performs the Visitation Circumambulation that is the essential element. One then performs Traversal if one did not already do so. Everything [that was unlawful during pilgrimage] is now permissible ‹even women›.

وَسُنَّ أَنْ يَشْرَبَ مِنْ زَمْزَمَ لِمَا أَحَبَّ، وَيَتَضَلَّعَ مِنْهُ، وَيَدْعُوَ بِهَا وَرَدَ، ثُمَّ يَرْجِعَ فَيَبِيتُ بِمِنًى ثَلَاثَ لَيَالٍ، وَيَرْمِي اَلْجِمَارَ فِي كُلِّ يَوْمٍ مِنْ أَيَّامِ اَلتَّشْرِيقِ بَعْدَ اَلزَّوَالِ وَقَبْلَ اَلصَّلَاةِ، وَمَنْ تَعَجَّلَ فِي يَوْمَيْنِ، إِنْ لَمْ يَخْرُجْ قَبْلَ اَلْغُرُوبِ لَزِمَهُ اَلْمَبِيتُ وَالرَّمْيُ مِنَ اَلْغَدِ.

It is recommended that he drink water from the well of Zamzam [and to supplicate] for whatever one wishes. One drinks until full and then supplicates using the transmitted supplications ‹e.g.,

> "*bi-smi Llāhi, Allāhumma-jʿalhu lanā ʿilman nāfiʿan wa rizqan wāsiʿan wa rayyan wa karḍan wa shibʿan wa shifāan min kulli dā'in, wa-ghsil bihi qalbī wa-mla'hu min khashyatika wa ḥikmatika*"
>
> ("In the name of Allah. O Allah, grant us a knowledge that benefits, a sustenance that is abundant, moistening and fulfilling, and a cure from every affliction. Wash my heart with it, and fill it with awareness of You and with Your wisdom.)›.

One then returns and stays in Minā for three nights. One throws pebbles at the ‹three› pillars during each of the Days of Tashrīq [Dhu l-Ḥijjah 11–13] after the sun reaches its zenith and before praying the Noon Prayer.

Whoever hastens his departure [by leaving] after two days: if he did not leave before sunset, he is required to stay the night and throw [pebbles] the next day.

وَطَوَافُ ٱلْوَدَاعِ وَاجِبٌ يَفْعَلُهُ، ثُمَّ يَقِفُ فِي ٱلْمُلْتَزِمِ دَاعِيًا بِمَا وَرَدَ، وَتَدْعُو ٱلْحَائِضُ وَالنُّفَسَاءُ عَلَى بَابِ ٱلْمَسْجِدِ.

The Farewell Circumambulation is an obligation. One performs it and then stands in the Black Stone's corner and the door [*al-multazam*] and makes a supplication that has been transmitted ‹e.g.,

> ‹"*Allāhumma hādha baytuka wa anā ʿabduka wa-bnu ʿabdika wa-bnu amatika, ḥamaltanī ʿalā mā sakhkharta lī min khalqika, wa sayyartanī fī bilādika ḥattā ballaghtanī bi-niʿmatika ilā baytika, wa aʿantanī ʿalā adā'i nusukī fa-in kunta raḍīta ʿannī fa-zdad ʿannī riḍan, wa illā fa-munna*

> *qabla an tana'ā ʿan baytika dārī wa hādha awānu-nṣirāfī in adhinta lī ghayru mustabdilan bika wa lā baytika wa lā rāghibin ʿanka wa lā ʿan baytika, Allāhumma fa aṣḥibnī l-ʿāfiyata fī badanī wa-ṣ-ṣiḥḥati fī jismī wa-l-ʿiṣmata fī dīnī wa aḥsin munqalabī, war-zuqnī ṭāʿataka mā abqaytanī, wa-jmaʿ lī bayna khayrayi d-dunyā wa-l-ākhurati innaka ʿalā kulli shay'in qadīr*"
>
> ("O Allah, this is Your house, and I am Your servant the son of Your two servants. You have carried me on one of Your creatures that You have made submissive to me, bringing me to Your land until, by Your grace, I reached Your House, and You graced me that I might fulfill Your rites. If you are pleased with me then be more so, and if not, then bless me now before I become distant from Your House – my house. Now is the time I depart if You permit me, who seek none but You and no other than Your house, and am not averse to You or Your house. O Allah, give me good health in body and protect me in my religion. Make my affairs turn out well and give me sustenance of obedience to You as long as You let me live. Give me the best of this world and the next, for truly You have power over everything.")›.

A woman with menstruation or lochia supplicates from the gate of the mosque.

وَسُنَّ زِيَارَةُ قَبْرِ ٱلنَّبِيِّ ﷺ وَقَبْرَيْ صَاحِبَيْهِ.

It is recommended to visit the grave of the Prophet ﷺ and the graves of his two companions (may Allah be pleased with them).

وَصِفَةُ ٱلْعُمْرَةِ: أَنْ يُحْرِمَ بِهَا مَنْ بِالْحَرَمِ مِنْ أَدْنَى ٱلْحِلِّ، وَغَيْرُهُ مِنْ دُوَيْرَةِ أَهْلِهِ، إِنْ كَانَ دُونَ ٱلْمِيقَاتِ، وَإِلَّا فَمِنْهُ، ثُمَّ يَطُوفُ وَيَسْعَى وَيُقَصِّرُ.

The description of [performing] Umrah is that anyone in the Sacred Precinct enters the state of pilgrimage [*iḥrām*] from the closest point outside the Sacred Precinct [*adnā al-ḥill*] and that others enter it from his homeland [*duwayrah ahilihi*] if it is closer than the appointed points of entry [*mīqāt*]. Otherwise, he enters from the appointed place of entry. One then performs Circumambulation, Traversal, and shortening the hair.

Essential & Obligatory Elements of Hajj & Umarah

(فَصْلٌ) أَرْكَانُ ٱلْحَجِّ أَرْبَعَةٌ: إِحْرَامٌ، وَوُقُوفٌ، وَطَوَافٌ، وَسَعْيٌ.

The essential elements of Hajj are four:
‹1› entering the state of pilgrimage [*iḥrām*];
‹2› standing ‹on ʿArafah›;
‹3› Circumambulation; and,
‹4› traversal ‹between Ṣafā and Marwah›.

وَوَاجِبَاتُه سَبْعَةٌ: إِحْرَامُ مَارٍّ عَلَى مِيقَاتٍ مِنْهُ، وَوُقُوفٌ إِلَى ٱللَّيْلِ إِنْ وَقَفَ نَهَارًا، وَمَبِيتٌ بِمُزْدَلِفَةَ إِلَى بَعْدِ نِصْفِهِ، إِنْ وَافَاهَا قَبْلَهُ، وَبِمِنَى لَيَالِيهَا، وَالرَّمْيُ مُرَتَّبًا، وَحَلْقٌ أَوْ تَقْصِيرٌ، وَطَوَافُ وَدَاعٍ.

Its obligatory elements are seven:
‹1› that anyone passing an appointed place of entry [*mīqāt*] enter the state of pilgrimage from it;
‹2› standing ‹on ʿArafah› until night for anyone who stood during the day;
‹3–4› staying the night at Muzdalifah until after half ‹the night› if one arrived before it, and in Minā during its nights;
‹5› throwing ‹stones at the pillars› in order;
‹6› shaving or trimming [the head]; and,
‹7› the Farewell Circumambulation.

وَأَرْكَانُ ٱلْعُمْرَةِ ثَلَاثَةٌ إِحْرَامٌ، وَطَوَافٌ، وَسَعْيٌ.

The essential elements of Umrah are three:
‹1› entering the state of pilgrimage;
‹2› Circumambulation; and,
‹3› traversal.

وَوَاجِبَاتُهَا اِثْنَانِ: اَلْإِحْرَامُ مِنَ اَلْحِلِّ، وَالْحَلْقُ أَوْ اَلتَّقْصِيرُ.

Its obligatory elements are two:
‹1› entering the state of pilgrimage from outside the Sacred Precinct [*al-ḥill*]; and,
‹2› shaving or trimming [the head].

وَمَنْ فَاتَهُ اَلْوُقُوفُ فَاتَهُ اَلْحَجُّ، وَتَحَلَّلَ بِعُمْرَةٍ وَهَدْيٍ إِنْ لَمْ يَكُنْ اِشْتَرَطَ.

Whoever missed standing ‹on ʿArafah› has missed Hajj. He is released [from his rites] by performing Umrah and making a *hadī* sacrifice[1] if he did not make a stipulation [for release] .

وَمَنْ مُنِعَ اَلْبَيْتَ هَدَى ثُمَّ حَلَّ، فَإِنْ فَقَدَهُ صَامَ عَشْرَةَ أَيَّامٍ، وَمَنْ صُدَّ عَنْ عَرَفَةَ تَحَلَّلَ بِعُمْرَةٍ وَلَا دَمَ.

Whoever was prevented from the House ‹i.e., entering the Sacred Precinct› makes a *hadī* sacrifice and is then released [from the rites]. If he does not have a sacrifice, he fasts ten days.

Whoever was blocked from [standing on] ʿArafah is released by performing Umrah and no blood [sacrifice is required].

‹If everyone making Hajj or all except a few stand on ʿArafah on the 8th or 10th of Dhi l-Ḥijjah by mistake, it suffices them.›

1. A *hadī sacrifice* refers to an animal brought to the Sacred Precinct specifically for that purpose. An *uḍḥiyah* sacrifice refers to an animal slaughtered on the day of Eid.

Sacrifice

(فَصْلٌ) وَالْأُضْحِيَةُ سُنَّةٌ، يُكْرَهُ تَرْكُهَا لِقَادِرٍ.

The *uḍḥiyah* sacrifice is recommended, and it is offensive for someone able to do so to omit it.

وَوَقْتُ اَلذَّبْحِ: بَعْدَ صَلَاةِ اَلْعِيدِ أَوْ قَدْرِهَا إِلَى آخِرِ ثَانِي اَلتَّشْرِيقِ.

The time for slaughtering is from after Eid Prayer or its amount, up until the second Day of Tashrīq [Dhu l-Ḥijjah 12].

وَلَا يُعْطَى جَازِرٌ أُجْرَتَهُ مِنْهَا، وَلَا يُبَاعُ جِلْدُهَا وَلَا شَيْءٌ مِنْهَا بَلْ يُنْتَفَعُ بِهِ.

The slaughterer is not given his wages from the animal, nor its hide or any other portion of it sold. Rather, they are benefited from.

وَأَفْضَلُ هَدْيٍ وَأُضْحِيَّةٍ: إِبِلٌ، ثُمَّ بَقَرٌ، ثُمَّ غَنَمٌ.

What is best for *hadī* and *uḍḥiyah* sacrifices is a camel, [then a] cow, and then a sheep.

وَلَا يُجْزِئُ إِلَّا جِذْعُ ضَأْنٍ أَوْ ثَنِيُّ غَيْرِهِ، فَثَنِيُّ إِبِلٍ مَا لَهُ خَمْسُ سِنِينَ، وَبَقَرٍ سَنَتَانِ، وَتُجْزِئُ اَلشَّاةُ عَنْ وَاحِدٍ، وَالْبَدَنَةُ وَالْبَقَرَةُ عَنْ سَبْعَةٍ، وَلَا تُجْزِئُ هُزَيْلَةٌ وَبَيِّنَةُ عَوَرٍ أَوْ عَرَجٍ، وَلَا ذَاهِبَةُ اَلثَّنَايَا، أَوْ أَكْثَرِ أُذُنِهَا أَوْ قَرْنِهَا.

وَالسُّنَّةُ نَحْرُ إِبِلٍ قَائِمَةً مَعْقُولَةً يَدُهَا اَلْيُسْرَى وَذَبْحُ غَيْرِهَا، وَيَقُولُ: «بِسْمِ اَللهِ اَللَّهُمَّ هَذَا مِنْكَ وَلَكَ».

Nothing suffices ‹for an obligatory *hadī* or *uḍḥiyyah*› except for a six-month-old male sheep [*jadhᶜ ḍa'n*], or a one-year-old [*thaniy*] of something else. ‹The *thaniy* is a goat that has completed one full year.› The *thaniy* of a camel has five years, and of a cow two. A single sheep suffices [as *hadī* or *uḍhiyyah*] for an individual ‹and his household and his family›, while a camel and a cow suffice for seven [individuals and their households and families].

[A sacrificial animal] that is emaciated, or clearly one-eyed or lame does not suffice. Neither does one that is missing its front teeth, most of an ear, or its horn.

It is recommended to slaughter a camel from the bottom of its neck while it is standing and with its left leg hobbled. Other animals are slaughtered from the top of the neck. One says "*Bismi Llāhi, Allāhumma hādhā minka wa laka*" ("In the name of Allah. O Allah, this is from You and for You").

وَسُنَّ أَنْ يَأْكُلَ وَيُهْدِيَ وَيَتَصَدَّقَ أَثْلَاثًا مُطْلَقًا وَالْحَلْقُ بَعْدَهَا، وَإِنْ أَكَلَهَا إِلَّا أُوقِيَّةً
جَازَ، وَحَرُمَ عَلَى مُرِيدِهَا أَخْذُ شَيْءٍ مِنْ شَعْرِهِ، وَظُفْرِهِ وَبَشَرَتِهِ فِي الْعَشْرِ.

It is recommended ‹for one making a sacrifice› to eat, gift, and give charity [from the sacrifice] – one-third each ‹i.e., he and his household eat one third, gift with one third, and give charity with one third›, categorically [*muṭlaqan*] ‹whether obligatory or not. It is permissible to give meat from a voluntary sacrifice to a non-Muslim›.

‹It is recommended to give charity from the best of it, gift the average of it, and eat the least of it.›

‹It is recommended› to shave afterward. If one eats all of it except for an *ūqiyah* [118.58 grams], it is permissible. It is unlawful for someone who intends to perform a sacrifice to removes any of his hair, nails, or skin during the ten days of Dhi l-Ḥijjah.

Slaughtering for a Newborn

وَتُسَنُّ الْعَقِيقَةُ وَهِيَ عَنِ الْغُلَامِ شَاتَانِ، وَعَنِ الْجَارِيَةِ شَاةٌ تُذْبَحُ يَوْمَ السَّابِعِ،
فَإِنْ فَاتَ فَفِي أَرْبَعَةَ عَشَرَ، فَإِنْ فَاتَ فَفِي أَحَدَ وَعِشْرِينَ، ثُمَّ لَا تُعْتَبَرُ الْأَسَابِيعُ،
وَحُكْمُهَا كَأُضْحِيَّةٍ.

Slaughtering for a newborn [*ʿaqīqah*] is recommended: two sheep for a male, and one for a female. It is slaughtered on the seventh day. If missed, then on the fourteenth. If that is missed, then on the twenty-first. Then, increments of seven days are not significant ‹after this, so one slaughters on whatever day he wishes›.

Its ruling is like the ruling of an *uḍḥiyah* sacrifice.

7

JIHAD

كِتَابُ الجِهَادِ

هُوَ فَرْضُ كِفَايَةٍ، إِلَّا إِذَا حَضَرَهُ أَوْ حَصَرَهُ أَوْ بَلَدَهُ عَدُوٌّ، أَوْ كَانَ النَّفِيرُ عَامًّا فَفَرْضُ عَيْنٍ، وَلَا يَتَطَوَّعُ بِهِ مَنْ أَحَدُ أَبَوَيْهِ حُرٌّ مُسْلِمٌ إِلَّا بِإِذْنِهِ.

Jihad is a communal obligation [*farḍ*] except when someone is present ‹in the battle line›, or he or his land has been encircled, or there is a general call to arms – then it is a personal obligation.

One does not voluntarily participate if one of one's parents is a free Muslim, except with their permission.

وَسُنَّ رِبَاطٌ وَأَقَلُّهُ سَاعَةٌ، وَتَمَامُهُ أَرْبَعُونَ يَوْمًا.

It is recommended to participate in manning border defenses [*ribāṭ*]. Its minimum duration is one hour; its complete duration is forty days.

‹[The following sections concerning emigration and prisoners of war are added here since it will be referenced later and this is where it originally occurs in the commentary.]

وَالْهِجْرَةُ وَاجِبَةٌ عَلَى كُلِّ مَنْ عَجَزَ عَنْ إِظْهَارِ دِيْنِهِ بِمَحَلٍّ يَغْلِبُ فِيهِ حُكْمُ الْكُفْرِ وَالبِدَعِ المُضِلَّةِ.

فَإِن قَدِرَ عَلَى إِظْهَارِ دِيْنِهِ فَمَسْنُوْنَةٌ فِي حَقِّهِ لِيَتَخَلَّصَ من تَكْثِيرِ الْكُفَّارِ وَمُخَالَطَتِهِمْ وَلِيَتَمَكَّنَ مِن جِهَادِهِمْ.

Emigration is an obligation upon every individual unable to practice his religion in public from a place where the rule of non-Muslims or misguided innovation dominates. If one is able to display one's religion, then for him [emigration] is recommended in order to remove oneself from augmenting the non-Muslims and mingling with them, and in order to be prepared to make jihad against them.

وَالْأُسَارَى مِنْهُم عَلَى قِسْمَيْنِ: قِسْمٌ يَكُوْنُ رَقِيْقًا بِمُجَرَّد السبى وَهُمْ النِّسَاءُ وَالصِّبْيَانُ، وَقِسْمٌ لَا، وَهُمْ الرِّجَالُ البَالِغُوْنَ المُقَاتِلُون، وَالْإِمَامُ فِيْهِم مُخَيَّرٌ تَخْيِير مَصْلَحَةٍ وَاجْتِهَادٍ لِلْمُسْلِمِيْنَ لَا تَخْيِير شَهْوَةٍ بَيْنَ رِقٍّ وَقَتْلٍ وَمَنٍّ وَفِدَاءٍ بِمَالٍ أَوْ بِأَسِيْرٍ مُسْلَم، وَيَجِبُ عَلَيْهِ اخْتِيَارُ الْأَصْلَحِ فَلَا يَجُوْزُ عُدُوْلٌ عَمَّا رَآهُ مَصْلَحَةً، فَإِنْ تَرَدَّدَ نَظَرُهُ فَقَتْلٌ أَوْلَى،

Non-Muslim prisoners of war are in two categories. One category is enslaved automatically by virtue of being taken prisoner; they are women and children. One category is *not* [automatically enslaved]; they are mature male combatants. Concerning them, the Imam chooses based on public welfare [*maṣlaḥah*] and personal reasoning [*ijtihād*] for the sake of the Muslims – not based upon lust. [He] chooses between enslavement; execution; and ransoming for money or exchanging for Muslim prisoners of war. It is obligatory for the Imam to choose what is in the best interest of welfare. It is not permissible for him to deviate from what he sees to be best for welfare. If his opinion keeps changing, killing them is best.

وَلَا يقتل صبي وَأُنْثَى وَخُنْثَى وراهب وَشَيخ فان وزمن أعمى لَا رأى لَهُم وَلم يقاتلوا ويحرضوا على الْقِتَال. وَإِن تترس الْكفَّار بهم رموا بِقصد المُقَاتلَة لَا إِن تترسوا بِمُسلم إِلَّا إِن خيف علينا، ويقصد الْكفَّار بِالرَّمْي دون الْمُسلم.

[The following] are not to be killed: minors, females, hermaphrodites, monks [or nuns], the elderly or the blind who have no say in it, did not fight, and did not encourage [others] to fight. If non-Muslims use them [i.e., the individuals just mentioned who are not to be killed] as shields, they are fired upon with the intent [to strike] the combatants. [But this is] not done if they use a Muslim as a shield – unless we fear for ourselves, and then the intent is [to strike] the non-Muslims and not the Muslim....›

وَعَلَى ٱلْإِمَامِ مَنْعُ مُخَذِّلٍ وَمُرْجِفٍ، وَعَلَى ٱلْجَيْشِ طَاعَتُهُ وَالصَّبْرُ مَعَهُ.

The Imam must prevent deserters and demoralizers. The army must obey the Imam and be patient with him.

وَتُمْلَكُ ٱلْغَنِيمَةُ بِالِاسْتِيلَاءِ عَلَيْهَا فِي دَارِ حَرْبٍ، فَيُجْعَلُ خُمُسُهَا خَمْسَةَ أَسْهُمٍ: سَهْمٌ لِلّٰهِ وَلِرَسُولِهِ، وَسَهْمٌ لِذَوِي ٱلْقُرْبَى وَهُمْ بَنُو هَاشِمٍ وَالْمُطَّلِبِ، وَسَهْمٌ لِلْيَتَامَى ٱلْفُقَرَاءِ، وَسَهْمٌ لِلْمَسَاكِينِ، وَسَهْمٌ لِأَبْنَاءِ ٱلسَّبِيلِ. وَشُرِطَ فِيمَنْ يُسْهَمُ لَهُ إِسْلَامٌ.

Enemy resources [*ghanīmah*] are owned by being confiscated in enemy lands. One-fifth of the spoils is divided into five shares: one share for Allah and His Messenger [ﷺ]; one for [his] relatives: Banī Ḥāshim and al-Muṭṭalib; one for poor orphans; one for the poor; and one for wayfarers. Being Muslim is a condition for recipients of shares.

ثُمَّ يُقْسَمُ ٱلْبَاقِي بَيْنَ مَنْ شَهِدَ ٱلْوَقْعَةَ: لِلرَّاجِلِ سَهْمٌ، وَلِلْفَارِسِ عَلَى فَرَسٍ عَرَبِيٍّ ثَلَاثَةٌ، وَعَلَى غَيْرِهِ اِثْنَانِ. وَيُقْسَمُ لِحُرٍّ مُسْلِمٍ وَيُرْضَخُ لِغَيْرِهِمْ.

The remainder is distributed between those who participated in the battle. A foot-soldier receives one share; a cavalryman mounted on an Arabian horse receives three shares and ‹one mounted› on another type of horse receives two shares.

‹The spoils› are distributed to free male Muslims. Others can receive a prize ‹less than the amount of a single share›.

وَإِذَا فَتَحُوا أَرْضًا بِالسَّيْفِ خُيِّرَ ٱلْإِمَامُ بَيْنَ قَسْمِهَا وَوَقْفِهَا عَلَى ٱلْمُسْلِمِينَ، ضَارِبًا عَلَيْهَا خَرَاجًا مُسْتَمِرًّا، يُؤْخَذُ مِمَّنْ هِيَ فِي يَدِهِ.

When a land is conquered by the sword ‹i.e., by force; e.g., the Levant, Iraq, and Egypt›, the Imam chooses between distributing it and declaring it an endowment for Muslims by putting a permanent levy on it that is taken from whoever holds it.

وَمَا أُخِذَ مِنْ مَالِ مُشْرِكٍ بِلَا قِتَالٍ كَجِزْيَةٍ وَخَرَاجٍ وَعُشْرٍ فَيْءٌ لِمَصَالِحِ ٱلْمُسْلِمِينَ، وَكَذَا خُمُسُ خُمُسِ ٱلْغَنِيمَةِ.

Anything taken from the wealth of polytheists without fighting (like *jizyah,* and the tenth ‹taken from non-Muslim traders who are from lands hostile to Islam, and the one-twentieth taken from a non-Muslim resident›) is tribute [*fay'*]: it is used for Muslim public welfare – as is the fifth of a fifth [taken] from the enemy resources [*ghanīmah*].

The Dhimmah Contract

(فَصْلٌ) وَيَجُوزُ عَقْدُ ٱلذِّمَّةِ لِمَنْ لَهُ كِتَابٌ أَوْ شُبْهَتُهُ وَيُقَاتَلُ هَؤُلَاءِ حَتَّى يُسْلِمُوا أَوْ يُعْطُوا ٱلْجِزْيَةَ، وَغَيْرُهُمْ حَتَّى يُسْلِمُوا أَوْ يُقْتَلُوا، وَيُؤْخَذُ مِنْهُمْ مُمْتَهَنِينَ مُصَغَّرِينَ، وَلَا تُؤْخَذُ مِنْ صَبِيٍّ وَعَبْدٍ وَامْرَأَةٍ وَفَقِيرٍ عَاجِزٍ عَنْهَا وَنَحْوِهِمْ.

The Dhimmah contract is permissible ‹for the Imam or his deputy only – and it is not valid from anyone else› with anyone who has a book of revelation or what resembles it ‹like the Zoroastrians [*Majūs*]›. They are fought until they enter Islam or give the *jizyah*. Others are fought until they enter Islam or are killed. The *jizyah* is taken from them "***mumtahanīn muṣaghgharīn***" ‹having to stand a long time with their arms outstretched›. It is not taken from a minor, slave, woman, someone too poor to pay it, or the like ‹e.g., someone who is blind, elderly, insane, decrepit, or a monk in a monastery›.

وَيَلْزَمُ أَخْذُهُمْ بِحُكْمِ ٱلْإِسْلَامِ فِيمَا يَعْتَقِدُونَ تَحْرِيمَهُ مِنْ نَفْسٍ وَعِرْضٍ وَمَالٍ وَغَيْرِهَا.

It requires that they be held accountable to Islamic law in things they consider unlawful, including life, dignity [ʿirḍ], property, and the like ‹e.g., theft›.

وَيَلْزَمُهُمُ ٱلتَّمَيُّزُ عَنِ ٱلْمُسْلِمِينَ، وَلَهُمْ رُكُوبُ غَيْرِ خَيْلٍ بِغَيْرِ سَرْجٍ.

They are required to be distinctive from Muslims. They can ride animals other than horses [but] without a saddle.

وَحَرُمَ تَعْظِيمُهُمْ، وَبُدَاءَتُهُمْ بِالسَّلَامِ.

It is unlawful to aggrandize them by greeting them with "*as-salāmu ʿalaykum.*"

وَإِنْ تَعَدَّى ٱلذِّمِّيُّ عَلَى مُسْلِمٍ، أَوْ ذَكَرَ ٱللهَ أَوْ كِتَابَهُ، أَوْ رَسُولَهُ بِسُوءٍ ٱنْتَقَضَ عَهْدُهُ، فَيُخَيَّرُ ٱلْإِمَامُ فِيهِ كَأَسِيرٍ حَرْبِيٍّ.

A *dhimmī* has broken his contract if he assaults a Muslim; or says something evil about Allah, the Quran, or His Messenger ﷺ. [In such a case,] the Imam chooses the same way he does with an enemy prisoner of war ‹as mentioned at the beginning of the chapter›.

[This ends the first portion of the book. The next chapter concerns sales and other financial transactions.]

This page left blank.

BIBLIOGRAPHY

المَصَادِرُ وَالمَرَاجِعُ

al-Baʿlī. *Kashf al-Mukhaddarāt wa al-Riyāḍ al-Muzhirāt li Sharḥ Akhṣar al-Mukhtaṣarāt*. Edited by Muḥammad Nāsir al-ʿAjmiy, 2 volumes. Beirut: Dār al-Bashāʾir al-Islāmiyyah, 1423/2002.

Ibn Balbān, Muḥammad. *Akhṣar al-Mukhtaṣarāt fī l-Fiqh ʿalā Madhhab al-Imām Aḥmad bin Ḥanbal*. Edited by Muḥammad Nāsir al-ʿAjmiy. Beirut: Dār al-Bashāʾir al-Islāmiyyah, 1416/1996.

al-Maqdasī, Muwaffaq al-Dīn ʿAbd Allāh bin Aḥmed bin Muḥammad bin Qudāmah. *Al-Mughnī*. 10 volumes. Cairo: Maktabat al-Qāhirah, 1388/1968.

al-Mardāwī, ʿAlī. *Al-Inṣāf fī Maʿrifat al-Rājiḥ min al-Khilāf*. Dār Iḥyāʾ al-Turāth al-ʿArabī, n.d.

al-Qaddūmī, Mūsā bin ʿĪsā. *Al-Ajwibatu l-Jaliyyatu fī l-Aḥkāmi l-Ḥanbaliyyah*. Translated by Joe Bradford as *Qaddūmīs Elementary Ḥanbali Primer*. CreateSpace, 2013.

ʿUthmān bin ʿAbd Allāh bin [Jumʿah bin] Jāmiʿ al-Ḥanbali, *Al-Fawāid al-Muntakhabāt fī Sharḥ Akhṣar al-Mukhtaṣarāt*. Edited by ʿAbd al-Salām bin Barjas Āl ʿAbd al-Karīm, 2 volumes. Beirut, Muʾassisat al-Risālah, 1424/2003.

ʿUthmān bin ʿAbd Allāh bin Jumʿah bin Jāmiʿ al-Ḥanbali, *Al-Fawāid al-Muntakhabāt fī Sharḥ Akhṣar al-Mukhtaṣarāt*. Edited by Khālid ʿAbd Allāh bin Shuʿayb and Jabīb Allāh Kamālī Muḥammad, 2 volumes. Riyadh: Maktabat al-Rushd, 1424/2003.

DETAILED TABLE OF CONTENTS

المُحْتَوَيَاتُ المُفَصَّلَةُ

PREFACE, IX

INTRODUCTION, 1

1 PURIFICATION, 3
Categories of Water, 3
Containers and Animals, 4
Going to the Lavatory, 5
The Toothstick and Other Sunnahs of the Body, 7
Obligatory and recommended acts of ablution, 8
Wiping over Footgear, 10
Ablution Invalidators, 12
Occasions Obligating the Purificatory Bath, 13
Dry Ablution, 15
Cleaning and Removing Filth, 18
Menstruation, 20

2 PRAYER, 23
Prayer Times, 23
The Call to Prayer, 24
Conditions for the Validity of Prayer, 25
Description of the Prayer, 30
Its Essential & Obligatory Elements, 38
The Prostration of Forgetfulness, 39
Voluntary Prayers, 41
Times wherein prayer is prohibited, 44
Congregational Prayer, 45
Imams, 46
People Who Have Excuses, 50
Travel and Peril, 50

Friday Prayer, 52
Eid Prayer, 56
Eclipse & Drought Prayers, 58

3 FUNERALS, 62
Sickness and Death, 62
Washing and Shrouding the Deceased, 63
The Funeral Prayer, 65
Carrying and Burying the Deceased, 68

4 ZAKAT, 72
Agriculture, 75
Gold and Silver, 76
Using Gold and Silver, 76
Trade Goods, 77
Al-Fiṭrah Alms, 77
Alms Payment, 78
Voluntary Charity, 80

5 FASTING, 81
The Intention to Fast, 82
Fast Invalidators, 82
Recommended Fasts, 85
Spiritual Retreat, 86

6 PILGRIMAGE, 88
The Mīqāt and Things Unlawful During Pilgrimage, 91
Expiations & Compensations, 94
Entering Mecca, 96
How to Perform Hajj and Umrah, 99
Essential & Obligatory Elements of Hajj & Umarah, 104
Sacrifice, 106
Slaughtering for a Newborn, 107

7. JIHAD, 109
The Dhimmah Contract, 112

BIBLIOGRAPHY, 115

ABOUT THE TRANSLATOR

Musa Furber is qualified to issue Islamic legal edicts (*fatwās*). He received his license to deliver edicts from senior scholars at the Egyptian House of Edicts (*Dār al-Iftā' al-Miṣriyyah*) including the Grand Mufti of Egypt. He studied traditional Islamic disciplines for over 15 years with numerous scholars in Damascus, Cairo, and elsewhere. He also holds a BA in Applied Linguistics from Portland State University, and an MPA from Dubai School of Government. He currently resides in Abu Dhabi, UAE.

www.ingramcontent.com/pod-product-compliance
Lightning Source LLC
Chambersburg PA
CBHW021154080526
44588CB00008B/331
* 9 7 8 1 9 4 4 9 0 4 0 3 6 *